Wanderings in
the Land of Mist

Wanderings in the Land of Mist

The Complete Story of Mussoorie

ANMOL JAIN

RUPA

First published by
Rupa Publications India Pvt. Ltd 2023
7/16, Ansari Road, Daryaganj
New Delhi 110002

Sales Centres:

Bengaluru Chennai
Hyderabad Jaipur Kathmandu
Kolkata Mumbai Prayagraj

P-ISBN: 978-93-5702-544-7
E-ISBN: 978-93-5702-543-0

First impression 2023

10 9 8 7 6 5 4 3 2 1

The moral right of the author has been asserted.

Printed in India

CONTENTS

To my dear father
Late Shri S.P. Jain

PREFACE

When my great-grandfather migrated to Mussoorie in 1901 to join the Alliance Bank of Simla—trudging up a narrow trail from Doon to Mussoorie and accosted by bitter cold and incessant rains—he would never have imagined that his family would continue living in this town for more than a century. Such is the charm of this hill station that despite all its shortcomings, no one wants to leave this place.

Perhaps it is the cool climate that is a welcome relief from the scorching heat of the plains or the scenic vistas that bewitch visitors. Or perhaps it is a combination of both that allured Captain Frederick Young and Frederick J. Shore to build a shooting box here in 1823 that ultimately paved the way for one of the most sought-after hill stations of the British era. A quaint little town that lay in close proximity to the plains had the 'grass-widows' flocking to during the summers with innumerable young suitors in pursuit. No wonder Mussoorie soon got the name 'the pleasure capital of the Raj'.

Over the years, Mussoorie has catered to all and sundry. During the pre-independence era, it was a summer haven for British army officers and their families, for rajas and maharajas of various princely states of India and a place of business for British and Indian traders. In Independent India, Mussoorie has witnessed a spurt of migrants from various parts of the country—some in search of rest and some in search of business. The town has opened its doors to everyone, rarely disappointing anyone.

This book captures the complete history of the town and brings to light extremely interesting yet lesser-known facts about the town—the first construction; how the town and places across the town were named; folklores about the stay of Balram (brother of Lord Krishna) on a hill to the west of town and his ancient idol; Sir George Everest's stay and his frequent tiffs with Captain Young, the founding father; the first burial and a history of cemeteries and the distinguished people buried; how it became the 'pleasure capital' for the British; the numerous scandals of the nineteenth and the twentieth centuries; the first church of Himalayas; the first brewery in the hills and the brewing tradition; India's second hydropower plant and the second electricity-run cinema hall of the country; the connection with the infamous General Dyer and with Mohan Meakin breweries of Uttar Pradesh; the 'human oil extractors' that tormented the residents; the schools and the Olympic hockey gold medallists...and much more.

I have meticulously researched numerous journals, travelogues and guidebooks dating back to the nineteenth and early twentieth centuries to present the readers with authentic and factual information. In addition, discussions with authors, historians and old-timers have helped in adding numerous anecdotes and tales of supernatural and mystery—some humorous and some awe-inspiring—which would captivate the attention of readers.

At the end of the book, a number of QR codes have been provided that can be used to navigate across the town to various places of tourist interest. I am sure tourists would find these QR codes quite useful.

1

ROOTS OF MUSSOORIE

'Such an influx of settlers reminds one of the gold-fields. Only in this case health, not wealth, was the magnet.'

—E.H. Ashworth[1]

They came searching for game and ended up founding one of India's most picturesque hill stations!

It was in 1823—two centuries ago—when two officers set foot on soil that would soon become the Britishers' getaway from the searing heat of the subcontinental plains and the administrative burden of managing the Indian empire—without a second thought, the dazzling jewel of the British crown.

Captain Frederick Young, accompanied by Superintendent of Dehradun F.J. Shore, went hunting in the hills adjoining Dehradun. They trekked up to the north of the Doon Valley, scrambling up narrow goat paths to reach a high ridge, where they were met with a stunning view. The valley sprawled beneath them, a rich and verdant canvas of untainted flora, bounded by the Shivalik peaks to the south; to the north, snow-clad mountain ranges shimmered in a soft, golden, balmy sunlight.

Game was abundant, the weather splendid—what more could the two hope for after stumbling upon uncharted territory? With time, their visits uphill became frequent. And soon, it was time to 'leave their mark' on the soon-to-be town of Mussoorie. The duo erected a 'shooting box' on a hill—not on the Camel's Back Road, but near the present-day Christ Church—facing the Doon Valley[2] (see

[1]Ashworth E.H., Report on the Land Tenures of Mussoorie (Allahabad: United Province Government Press, 1904), 2.

[2]Shakespeare L.W., History of the 2nd King Edward's Own Gurkha Rifles (Aldershot: Gale & Polden Ltd, 1912), 24.

Where was the 'shooting box' erected?

All the guide books on Mussoorie mention that the 'shooting box' by Young and Shore was constructed somewhere on Camel's Back Road.

But have our 'guides' misguided us? It seems so.

Rummaging through old records, I have found sufficient and reliable evidence that points out that this shooting box was on the hill facing Dehradun, near the site of the present-day Christ Church. Also, this was not a permanent structure.

In a 1912 book about the history of Gurkha Rifles, Colonel L.W. Shakespeare recounts the visit of Captain Mundy in 1827 to the shooting box: 'They paid Captain Young a visit to his little shooting box of ringall "and wattle and daub", which he and Shore shared on the site of the present church,' Shakespeare writes.

The location of the shooting box is further confirmed in an 1831 map of Mussoorie in which the shooting box is depicted at a little distance above Mall Road near present-day Christ Church.

---

box). This is considered the first piece of British construction on the hills that attracts millions of tourists from around the world today.

Captain Frederick Young, the founder of Mussoorie and Landour, also the founder of Sirmoor Rifles. He later became the superintendent of Dehradun and eventually retired as a General (Source: Shakespeare L. W., History of the 2nd King Edward's Own Gurkha Rifles, Aldershot: Gale and Polden Ltd., 1912, facing page 3)

Frederick John Shore, the joint magistrate and superintendent of Dehradun from 1823 to 1829 (Source: Ibid, facing page 27)

Before long, hordes of Europeans trudged up the hills of the horseshoe-shaped ridge, following eagerly in the footsteps of Young and Shore. (They might as well have named the town 'Young and Shore', but I'm glad they didn't. It would've sounded more like a departmental store chain in the heart of London than a calm town nestled in the hills in India.) The Europeans bore the same desires: to hunt and to absorb the stimulating climate.[3]

Formative Years

Today's Mussoorie is crowded, with buildings cropping up at every nook and corner, many even precariously perched atop steep slopes. But things were apparently much different in the formative years of this town, heavily forested slopes offered little scope to erect any kind of lodging.

It might be difficult to picture, but the bustling Mussoorie of today was carved out of pristine hill slopes. The Mussoorie of yesteryears comprised densely forested slopes, cradling lush canopies of deodar and oak. Come spring, crimson rhododendron flowers would break the monotony of endless green. The only semblance of any construction to be found were a few scattered huts belonging to villagers from nearby Kyar Kuli, Bhatta, Dudhli and some other villages.

Interestingly, the British empire did not own these hills. The ownership lay with: a) the Raja of Tehri Garhwal—of lands on the northern slopes of Mussoorie and Landour hills;[4] b) the Mahant of

---

[3]'Climate of Mussoorie is considered the most salubrious in India and of its good effects I can offer a practical illustration in my own person having grown excessively stout during the few weeks I have been here,' excerpt from a letter by Mauger Fitzhugh Monk, a teacher at Mussoorie Seminary School, to his father Hugh Monk, dated 13 April 1840. Monk M.F., *Letters of a Mussoorie Merchant* (New Delhi: Niyogi Books, 2011).

[4]The Rambler, *A Mussoorie Miscellany* (Mussoorie: Mafasilite Press, 1936), 23.

Guru Ram Rai shrine[5] at Dehradun—who owned lands to the east and also at the present-day Happy Valley area; and c) zamindars from nearby Kyar Kuli and Dudhli villages[6]—who owned a major part of the southern slopes of Mussoorie, including the present-day Mall Road, Jharipani, Barlowganj, and also Cloud's End and Hathipaon to the west.

As the Europeans lumbered up these hills, they looked to find suitable sites for their summer abodes. While the sloping mountain landscape offered little leeway for erecting any kind of lodging, their only option were the few 'flats'[7] where local villagers had built small hutments to house their cattle during the summers.[8]

There were around seven large 'flats' on the Mussoorie Ridge[9]: present-day Landour Cantonment—on the ridge above Lal Tibba, where the tennis courts used to be; Mullingar—at the end of the Landour Market, where the road forks to the right towards Tehri, and which became famous as the residence of Captain (later General) Young, the founding father of the town; Annfield—a little below and towards the left of Mullingar; Zephyr Lodge—a high hill in the present-day Kulri area of the town; Savoy Hotel—just behind the Mussoorie Library building at Gandhi Chowk; Happy Valley—below the present-day Lal Bahadur Shastri National Academy; Park Estate—in the extreme west-end of the town, where Sir George Everest went on to build his house.

---

[5]The name of the then mahant was Swarup Das.

[6]The villagers of Kyar Kuli and Dudhli villages near Mussoorie were the original owners of what is today the central part of Mussoorie. Their residential dwellings were in the villages down below, but they had also built small hutments scattered across the slopes of present-day Mussoorie where they brought their cattle to graze during the summers.

[7]Level lands with moderate or no slope

[8]The Rambler, *A Mussoorie Miscellany* (Mussoorie: Mafasilite Press, 1936), 13.

[9]Ashworth E.H., *Report on the Land Tenures of Mussoorie* (Allahabad: United Province Government Press, 1904), 2.

Besides, there were a number of smaller flats scattered across the town. Most notable among these are the present-day Fairlawn (in Jharipani); Sylverton (in Kulri); Bala Hissar (present-day Wynberg Allen); Sikandar Hall (near Barlowganj); Minerva (in Kulri) and a few others.

The large flats caught the fancy of European settlers. And thus began a 'rat-race' to own a property in these sublime hills. Most of the sought-after flats were owned by local village folk, and the Europeans 'constantly cajoled or badgered'[10] them to sell their lands. Many 'sahebs' deployed their servants to do the bargaining for them, promising them large tips if they were able to close the deals at low rates. The native zamindars had to eventually bow before the might of the empire, most of them receiving ridiculously low compensation in lieu of their lands.

The 'shooting box' remains the first construction by the Europeans on these hills. As for the first residence, the general perception is that

> **There were no 'bungalows' in Mussoorie**
>
> 'I don't believe you! There were large estates in Mussoorie, sprawling over acres of land with huge buildings, and you are telling me there were no bungalows,' countered an old timer when I made this statement.
>
> 'Sir, tell me the name of one house that ends with the word "bungalow" then?' I questioned.
>
> Dear readers, the Europeans preferred to call their hill abodes 'cottages' rather than 'bungalows'.
>
> We have innumerable 'cottages' (like Antlers Cottage, Craig Cottage, Dale View Cottage, Hope Cottage). There are also a number of 'villas' (like Irene Villa, Ivy Villa, Mary Villa, Spring Villa), and so many 'houses' (like Auchnegie House, Clarence House, Manor House, Oxford House).
>
> The reason is simple—'bungalow' was a term with colonial overtones, used for European houses across India, except in the hills, where *cottage* (or even *villa* or *house*, for that matter) was preferred, as the word 'cottage' suggested a small English country home with a sloping roof and chimneys.

[10]The Rambler, *A Mussoorie Miscellany* (Mussoorie: Mafasilite Press, 1936), 13.

An early nineteenth century painting of Mussoorie and Doon Valley from Landour.
One can see a few houses on the slope. Artist: G.F. White (Source: White, G.F., Views
in India, Chiefly Among the Himalaya Mountains, London and Paris: Fisher, Son and
Co., 1838, facing page 30)

it was Mullingar—built by Captain Young, and named after a town
in his native Ireland—but it was actually Zephyr Cottage, a small
cabin built atop a high hill, offering a 360-degree view of the hills.
This locality, teeming with a number of multi-story houses now, is
located near the Picture Palace at the end of the Mall Road. Zephyr
has now been changed to Zafar[11] to ease the pronunciation.

The construction of Mullingar was completed in 1826,
followed by White Park Forest (later known as Annfield). Dear
readers, don't be misled into imagining that this property had a
park or a forest! In fact, it was named after three chums, named
White, Park and Forest, who had built it.

Other early settlements were The Park (1827), built by a

---

[11]A narrow road going up a steep slope near the Bata showroom leads to Zephyr
Hall after a steep climb of about 5 minutes. This locality is now clustered with
houses and also a few hotels. Zephyr Hall of old is now pronounced as 'Zafar
Hall' and is even spelled as such.

Colonel Whyshe—later to be the residence of Sir George Everest, and Phoenix Lodge (1829).

The construction of a 'convalescent depot' for European soldiers, an idea floated by Young to his superiors in the army, was started at Landour in 1827, and made operational in 1829.[12] Mussoorie and Landour were initially two separate townships. Landour, with the convalescent depot atop the hill, was to the east of Mussoorie Ridge. Mussoorie was developing towards the west, in the direction of Hathipaon and Cloud's End. The first school and the first brewery were towards the west, and so were several early buildings, including The Park, Cloud's End, Leopard Lodge and Clover Lodge.

The heat-scorched Europeans were smitten by the salubrious mountain climate, and as word spread, prospective settlers swarmed these hills. Widespread diseases in the plain fuelled the migration. 'This desire was heightened by the devastating cholera epidemic that swept through India in 1817–1821.'[13]

The number of houses had increased to about 480 (340 European and 140 Indian residences) by 1882–1883, which swelled to 1,406 by 1935.[14] I earnestly endeavoured to find the number of houses at present, but miserably failed in the attempt. Under strict confidence, an official disclosed that there might be hundreds of illegal buildings in the town of which the municipality has no record! But just to give an indication to my readers, at present, there are around 4,200 residential and 1,200 commercial water connections in the town—and please

---

[12]Although, ailing soldiers (called 'invalids') had started to arrive much before the building was constructed.

[13]Arnold D., 'Cholera and Colonialism in British India', *Past & Present*, Vol 113, No. 1, 1 November 1986, 118–151. (c.f. Kennedy D., *Magic Mountains: Hills Stations and the British Raj*, Berkeley and Los Angeles: University of California Press, 1996, 20).

[14]The Rambler, *A Mussoorie Miscellany* (Mussoorie: Mafasilite Press, 1936), 41.

keep in mind that every building might not have a separate water connection.

Meanwhile, some residents of Rajpur[15] remain perpetually disappointed when they realize that they narrowly missed being a part of Mussoorie.

'Rajpur should have been a part of Mussoorie and not Dehradun! The hilly terrain starts from Rajpur, the bridle path to your town started from Rajpur, and as per the original boundaries drawn in early 1800s, Rajpur was a part of Mussoorie Municipality,' a disgruntled friend from Rajpur always argues.

It so happened that in the early part of the nineteenth century, Mussoorie's municipal limits extended to Rajpur (now part of Dehradun) with the total area being 27 square miles. Rajpur was later separated, and the total area of Mussoorie reduced to 19 square miles. In the 1920s, when plans were afoot to build a railway track up to Mussoorie, Rajpur was again brought under Mussoorie, but when this project failed Rajpur was yet again released from municipal control.

Early Businesses, Markets and Institutions

As the number of settlers swelled, along came a Jewish gentleman called Lawrence, perhaps the first entrepreneur to set foot in the budding town in 1829 with merchandise for the European community.

He hawked his goods around the town, and if anyone so much as glanced in his direction, the zealous salesman would shout, 'comin', 'comin', and rush towards them. Lawrence was

---

[15]Rajpur is a locality that is part of Dehradun's municipal corporation. The locality lies at the foothills of the Mussoorie Ridge, just a few miles below Jharipani. The original trek route to Mussoorie originated from Rajpur and, even today, a large number of nature enthusiasts take the 5 kilometre trek from Rajpur to Jharipani.

soon nicknamed 'comin'.[16] Until our salesman decided he had had enough! He promptly dropped his Jewish surname and rechristened himself Lawrence Cumming.

Lawrence's venture came to a full circle and within a few years, he managed to open a store on the Mall, at the site where currently the head post office is.

In 1830, Henry Bohle, a distiller from Meerut, rushed to the hills to take advantage of the cool climate and the wild yeast strains for brewing beer. Bohle wasn't successful in his first attempt at brewing, and a tiff with Captain Young forced him to shut down in 1832. But he did lay the roots for a successful brewery business in Mussoorie that continued till the end of the nineteenth century (see chapter 10).

Markets

As the 'invalids'[17] began to arrive at Landour's convalescent depot, a market appeared in the town (see chapter 2), primarily to cater to soldiers and other settlers. Shortly after this, the 'Kulri Bazaar'[18] was established, with shops near the present-day head post office and LIC building (erstwhile State Bank of India) and gradually the shops extended towards the present-day Picture Palace. A small market also came up at Char Dukan near St. Paul's Church,[19] although Landour Bazaar still remained the main market.

---

[16]The Rambler, *A Mussoorie Miscellany* (Mussoorie: Mafasilite Press, 1936), 16.
[17]A colloquial term used by the British for sick soldiers.
[18]Bodycot F., *Guide to Mussoorie* (Mussoorie: Mafasilite Printing Works, 1907), 31.
[19]Ibid.

A scene of the market on the Kulri slope. (Photo courtesy: Hotel Savoy, Mussoorie)

Early settlers living to the west of the town complained about having to travel several miles to access the markets and other conveniences located at Landour Bazaar. '...our post office is near seven miles from here and some eleven or twelve hundred feet higher than we are...'[20] writes Mauger Monk, a teacher at Masuri Seminary School located at Hathipaon.

This prompted F.O. Wells, the settlement officer, to assign an area of two acres for a market at Library[21] in 1842. The sites were allotted to merchants—most of them Europeans—in consideration of a rent of ₹1 for 120 square feet, payable to the municipal council. This market was referred to as 'Mussoorie Bazaar'.[22]

---

[20]Excerpt from a letter by Mauger Fitzhugh Monk to Isabella Monk dated 6 June 1840. Monk M.F., *Letters of a Mussoorie Merchant* (New Delhi: Niyogi Books, 2012), 28.

[21]Earlier known as 'Mussoorie Bazaar'.

[22]Bodycot F., *Guide to Mussoorie* (Mussoorie: Mafasilite Printing Works, 1907), 31.

Wells had also proposed a market at Hathipaon, but it seems that never materialized. In the meantime, a few shops also came up at Vincent Hill (called Upper Mussoorie Bazaar[23]), near Municipal Garden and also at Jabarkhet.

Early institutions

Within merely two decades of the arrival of the first Europeans, Mussoorie had grown at a rapid pace. As settlers swarmed, the founding fathers fretted about the need to develop civic amenities. In 1842, they requested the North-Western Provinces[24] government to introduce the Municipal Act[25] in Mussoorie. A twelve-member Mussoorie Municipal Committee was constituted in 1842—the first such body amongst the hill stations and among the earliest municipal bodies in India.[26]

Mr A. Macgregor, the first municipal secretary, set up a humble one-room office in present-day Kutchery. Bellevue Estate (present-day Radha Bhawan Estate) was purchased in 1871, and the building was renovated to host the municipal office and a town hall. After the promulgation of the North-Western Province and Oudh Municipalities Act in 1883, the Mussoorie Municipal Board was constituted.

In the early 1900s, a new municipal office building was

---

[23]Ibid.

[24]Mussoorie was part of North-Western Provinces, which was renamed 'United Provinces of Agra and Oudh' in 1902, and after 1947, to Uttar Pradesh.

[25]The first Municipal Act was passed in 1842, known as 'The Bengal Act X of 1842' for Bengal province only. It provided setting up of a town committee for looking after sanitary and other civic matters in the town. As a special case, the Uttar Pradesh Government introduced this act in Mussoorie (1842) and Nainital (1845). *Compendium of Urban Data* (Lucknow: Regional Centre for Urban and Environmental Studies, 2007).

[26]The first municipal body in India was the Fort Kochi municipality, established by the Dutch in 1664, followed by Madras Municipal Corporation in 1687, and Calcutta and Bombay corporations in 1776.

constructed near Kulri (at the present location), and the offices were shifted from Bellevue.

Post office

Postal services for soldiers at the Landour Cantonment started as early as 1827, although it took another ten years before the first post office began operating from Landour (see chapter 15). The father of legendary hunter-turned-conservationist Jim Corbett, Christopher William Corbett, served as the postmaster at Landour for many years! Several sub-post offices opened subsequently at Barlowganj, Hotel Savoy, Hotel Charleville and Jharipani. In 1909, the head post office was shifted to the Mall (at the present location), and the one at Landour was made a sub-post office.

Churches

Christ Church, constructed in 1836, was not only the first church in Mussoorie, but also in the Himalayas. It is located near Gandhi Chowk and was consecrated in 1839. In the subsequent years, several churches were established in the town, and by the early twentieth century, Mussoorie had as many as eight churches (see chapter 6).

Schools

After Henry Bohle shut down his brewery in 1832, his property was purchased by Mr Parsons and from him by Bohle's son-in-law, John Mackinnon. Mackinnon established Masuri Seminary School in 1834 at the site of the old brewery near Hathipaon. Regarded as the first school for Europeans in the Himalayas, the school continued at the site of the old brewery until 1850, when it was shifted to the site where Hotel Savoy currently is (see chapter 9).

Banks

Mussoori Bank (later North-West Bank), floated by three Europeans in 1840, was the first bank in Mussoorie. It went into liquidation in 1859 due to financial irregularities. Come to think of it, the town's banking sector was probably jinxed. During the nineteenth century and early twentieth century, several banks opened in Mussoorie, but most came to grief (see chapter 12).

The Mussoorie Library

Integral to the history of our town is the Mussoorie Library, which is housed in an iconic Victorian style building at Gandhi Chowk. The Mussoorie Library was made operational in 1843–1844 through subscriptions to meet the cost of the building and the cost of books.

The land upon which the building was constructed belonged to Major Edmund Swetenham, the then Commandant of the Landour Convalescent Depot (read about his love story in chapter 4). A Mussoorie Library committee was formed under the Chairmanship of Mr Vansittart, the then Superintendent of Dehradun (or Doon, as it was referred to then), and ₹2,500 was collected as subscription.

An early twentieth century postcard showing The Mussoorie Library. Notice the 'Band Stand' in front of the building, which was later shifted towards the left.

Land was purchased from Major Swetenham for ₹300 and the building was raised. The rest is history!

Acclaimed author and historian Mr Ganesh Saili informed me that the Mussoorie Library Trust was set up to manage the library, and this trust has been functioning till date. Mr Saili also happens to be the honorary secretary of this institution—no better person than him to be the custodian of the town's heritage.

This library is a treasure trove of more than 16,000 books that include old travelogues, surveys, journals and rare books. 'This library is a cathedral for the mind and a celebration of knowledge,' Mr Saili says.

I am told that nearly half a century ago, celebrated author Ruskin Bond, while working on a project for an international charity, wrote the famous book *Strange Men Strange Places* based on his research in this library.

The first-floor verandah of the library was once used as a restaurant by Hotel Savoy when a band used to play at the chowk.[27]

Membership of the library is open to the residents of Mussoorie. A temporary membership of one year is offered, and during this period the interest of the member is assessed and only genuinely interested persons are offered a permanent membership.

Clubs

Our town had two famous clubs, both established during the colonial era. Both of them have been lost in the sands of time, but it might be worthwhile to know more about them.

Himalaya Club

Himalaya Club was formed in 1841 with 148 members, and the town's founder Colonel Frederick Young[28] (he was still around in

---

[27]Kinney T., *The Echo Guide to Mussoorie* (Mussoorie: Echo Press, 1908), 71.
[28]Our Captain Young of 1823 had risen through the ranks to become a Colonel by 1841.

A late nineteenth century photograph of The Himalaya Club. One can make out the thatched roof. This building has not changed much over the past two centuries and a hotel is presently running in these premises. (Picture courtesy: Hotel Savoy, Mussoorie)

Dehradun) was the first president. It was very expensive, exclusive and naturally, in high demand.

Situated atop a steep ridge above the road that led to Landour, the club offered stunning views of snow peaks to the north and the Doon Valley to the south. '...on a clear day the eye commands one of the grandest scenes in the known world,' if we are to believe John Lang[29], a patron of the club.

The club had thirty-two rooms for bachelors and eleven family suites, a dining room, reading room, ballroom and a tennis court.[30] Ladies had a separate dining room and reading room. The club also had a billiards room and a card room, where members played

---

[29]Lang J., *The Himalaya Club* in Dickens C. (ed.), *Household Words: Vol. XV, Magazine No. 365*, 21 March 1857, 265.

[30]Bodycot F., *Guide to Mussoorie* (Mussoorie: Mafasilite Printing Works, 1907), 139.

for high stakes. And no wonder, to be let into the club, you'd have to be rich!

The rates for boarding and lodging were exorbitant, but a special discount of nearly 33 per cent was offered to those who did not mind a cold meal.

Lang was intrigued by the large stables at the club, which dug into the hillside. 'No horses, except those educated in India, would crawl into these holes cut out of the earth and rock,'[31] he observed.

Membership was open only for 'men' of European origin, and a new member was admitted only after the approval of existing members through a ballot. 'It was a terribly "select" institution and while merchants were permitted entry, mere tradesmen were tabooed! Such a vast distinction was perhaps, adjudged on whether one sold tin cans or tin cars,' wrote Williams[32] (1936).

By the early 1880s, the membership of the club had swelled to 759[33] (including 258 temporary members), and was regarded as one of the best clubs in India.[34]

The club closed down after World War I, and the property was put up for sale. It was purchased by an Indian businessman whose family now runs two hotels at this site.

Happy Valley Club

A racecourse in the mountains! Yes readers, as early as in the nineteenth century, there was a racecourse in Mussoorie—albeit small—at Happy Valley, a property owned by Mr Henry Vansittart, the then superintendent of Dehradun.

---

[31] Ibid.

[32] The Rambler, *A Mussoorie Miscellany* (Mussoorie: Mafasilite Press, 1936), 20.

[33] Northam J., *Guide to Masuri, Landaur, Dehradun and The Hills North of Dehra* (Calcutta: Thacker, Spink and Co., 1884), 53.

[34] Ibid, 34.

A late nineteenth century postcard showing the racecourse at Happy Valley. Hotel Charleville can be seen above the ridge on the right. The racecourse was replaced by Happy Valley Club after 1904. (Photographer: C. Nickels)

Happy Valley Estate was purchased by Vincent Mackinnon,[35] a rich brewer, in April 1904. Shortly thereafter, in a meeting held at Mussoorie Library, it was decided to establish an amusement club at Happy Valley.[36]

The club meant the death knell for Vansittart's racecourse as its area was taken over for developing tennis courts,[37] along with a billiards room, card room, reading room, a library and a field for cricket and hockey.

The Happy Valley Club gained immense popularity amongst the residents, especially those residing at the west-end of the town.

'The Happy Valley Club has been most successful and has

---

[35]He was the son of John Mackinnon. John opened the first school in Mussoorie, and later ran a successful brewery business.

[36]Kinney T., *The Echo Guide to Mussoorie* (Mussoorie: Echo Press, 1908), 71.

[37]There were fourteen tennis courts at Happy Valley Club. Walton H.G., *Dehradun, A Gazetteer: Vol. I of the District Gazetteers of the United Provinces of Agra and Oudh* (Allahabad: Government Press, 1911), 247.

proved a great boon...' a guidebook of 1908[38] observed.

But apparently, the Europeans did not fancy a club without equestrian sports. Soon, a hillside was dug up near Herne Del—about a mile below Happy Valley—to make way for a new racecourse and polo ground. Soon the 'Polo Ground' became quite popular for holding equestrian events, a 'gymkhana'.

The outbreak of World War II had its impacts upon the fortunes of the club. The last gymkhana was held at the Polo Ground on 19 June 1943 to raise funds for the Red Cross during the war.[39] In the subsequent years, the club was closed and the property put up for sale.

In 1959, a part of the Happy Valley Club was acquired by the government to establish the Lal Bahadur Shastri National Academy of Administration (LBSNAA) for training civil servants. A horse riding ground, a shooting range and the sports club of LBSNAA have come up on the premises of the erstwhile club.

It is but a paradox that the country's budding bureaucrats—the coveted IAS officer trainees at the LBSNAA—can now be seen gingerly trotting their horses near Vansittart's racecourse.

A major part of the erstwhile club is now a settlement for Tibetan refugees, who arrived in Mussoorie after their exodus from Tibet.

The Polo Ground is used by the youth for cricket and football matches and, occasionally, as a helipad for VIPs arriving at LBSNAA.

The story of double 's's and double 'o's

As a child, the spelling of our town befuddled me, and I faced a lot of flak from teachers who struggled to set it right.

[38]Kinney T., *The Echo Guide to Mussoorie* (Mussoorie: Echo Press, 1908), 70.
[39]'History', *Lal Bahadur Shastri National Academy of Administration*, 7 February 2023, https://www.lbsnaa.gov.in/cms/history.php

Mansur or Mansuri shrub after which Mussoorie is named.

'Why do you always forget that it is spelled with a double "s" and double "o",' Mrs Shepherd, my language teacher, would point out. I have since managed to learn that it is spelled 'Mussoorie' but never stopped wondering about the need for the double 's' followed by the double 'o'.

'Perhaps the name has a British, Irish or Scottish origin and hence the quirky spelling,' I'd muse.

Then, one of the old guidebooks came to my rescue! I was pleasantly surprised that our town's name has an Indian origin— named after a shrub called Mansur or Mansuri (botanical name *Coriaria nepalensis*), which was plentiful in these hills (not anymore, though). The native population called these hills 'Mansuri'[40] and the Europeans simply dropped the 'n'.[41] The town had a Masuri Hotel,[42] Masuri Volunteer Rifle Corps and even a culvert called Masuri khala.[43]

Over the years, the spelling of 'Masuri' was completely

---

[40]Walton H.G., *Dehradun, A Gazetteer: Vol. I of the District Gazetteers of the United Provinces of Agra and Oudh* (Allahabad: Government Press, 1911), 243.

[41]The Rambler, *A Mussoorie Miscellany* (Mussoorie: Mafasilite Press, 1936), 4.

[42]This now forms a part of Wynberg Allen School.

[43]Located near present-day Waverley Convent School.

distorted by the British, who you'll find had considerable trouble pronouncing and spelling Indian names. Over a major part of the nineteenth century, the town assumed various written forms: 'Masuri',[44] 'Mussoori'[45] and even 'Mussooree'.[46] The current spelling was made popular by a local advertisement bulletin, which started writing 'Masuri' as 'Mussoorie'.

As per *A Mussoorie Miscellany*[47], 'The Mussoorie Exchange Advertiser', which started in 1870, was merely a medium for advertisements but the 'semi-official murderer of the name "Masuri" replacing the victim with "Mussoorie".'

Old timers of the town lament that the Masuri shrub has retreated to the outskirts these days due to urbanisation, and that the younger generation has no clue about its contribution to the naming of the town.

Yours truly, along with a group of friends, tried to plant a few Masur trees along the Mall Road, but none of the saplings survived. So much for preserving our heritage.

---

[44]Fisher F.H., *Geological Sketch of Masuri and Landour in the Himalaya* (1832) and Northam J., *Guide to Masuri, Landaur, Dehradun and The Hills North of Dehra* (Calcutta: Thacker, Spink and Co., 1884).

[45]Parks F., *Wanderings of a Pilgrim in Search of the Picturesque: Vol. II* (London: Pelham Richardson, 1850), 224.

[46]Atkinson E.T., *The Himalayan Districts of the North-Western Provinces of India: Vol. 1. North-Western Provinces and Oudh* (Allahabad: Government Press, 1882), 299.

[47]The Rambler, *A Mussoorie Miscellany* (Mussoorie: Mafasilite Press, 1936), 30.

2

A TOWN WITHIN THE TOWN

In 1808, a few British officers[48], conducting a survey of river Ganga from Haridwar to Gaumukh, climbed the hills adjoining the Doon Valley and reached the Landour Ridge. From here they got 'their first look at the snow-clad Himalayan peaks'.[49]

'We had a good and extensive view of the Himalea[50] Mountains... The most remarkable peaks I delineated and took correct bearings of them, with a theodolite.' Hyder Jung Hearsey[51] wrote in his journal. It was a somewhat prosaic reference considering the circumstances; its significance is that it confirms Hearsey's presence at the spot.[52]

Little did Hearsey or other members of his party know that they had stumbled upon a piece of history. That the mesmerizing view of Himalayan peaks and the Doon Valley, as well as the benign climate, would make Landour (and Mussoorie, of course!) as one of the most sought-after hill destinations and that, centuries later, it would be home to who's who of the country.

---

[48]The exploration party was led by Lieutenant William Webb and comprised Captain Hyder Jung (later changed to Young) Hearsey and Captain Felix Raper.
[49]Allen C., *A Forgotten Pioneer of Himalayan Expedition* in Asian Affairs, Vol. XI, Part II (1980), 171.
[50]Notice the spelling
[51]Hyder Hearsey's grandson, Lionel Douglas Hearsey, settled down in these very hills at Maryville Estate in Barlowganj and established the famous Tivoli Garden in 1882—one of the most sought-after picnic destinations in Mussoorie. Tivoli Garden suffered huge damages during the 1905 earthquake and did not reopen.
[52]Allen C., *A Forgotten Pioneer of Himalayan Expedition* in Asian Affairs, Vol. XI, Part II (1980), 171.

An early nineteenth century painting of snow peaks as visible from Landour. Artist: G.F. White (Source: White G.F., Views in India, chiefly Among the Himalaya Mountains, London and Paris: Fisher, Son and Co., 1838, facing page 35)

Land-our, Landaura or Llanddowror?

I am always intrigued by the names of places. How 'Landour' got its name became yet another quest for me. I read and re-read old journals and guidebooks; had lengthy discussions with senior citizens; connected with several noted historians. Dear readers, the following is the outcome of all my efforts:

While one can pinpoint the origin of the name 'Mussoorie', the genesis of the name 'Landour' is still shrouded in mystery and various theories are floating around.

Seemingly 'ignorant' masses firmly believe that the British named it 'Land-our' to signify their ownership and control over this area and later, in common parlance, this came to be known as Landour. But I feel that the word 'Landour' is not a portmanteau.

Another theory, promulgated by various historians, is that

when the British depot was established here, a number of merchants (mostly Indian) also arrived, most of whom were from a place called Landhaura (near Roorkee).

My research also indicates that the name Landour could also have an English connection. Captain Mundy, a British soldier turned traveller, arrived here in 1828 and referred to Landour as Llandowr[53]—perhaps after a town called Llanddowror in Carmarthenshire, Wales. This may be true considering that there are several places in and around Mussoorie named after places in England, Ireland or Scotland. Although in his guide book, published nearly seventy-five years later, F. Bodycot ridiculed Mundy for this spelling: 'His spelling of Landour, which is retained, would seem to indicate that Capt. Mundy was a Welshman,'[54] Bodycot writes.

But I found the most convincing and the only documented evidence about how Landour got its name in a book by Lieutenant George Francis White that dates back to 1838.[55] According to White, there was a village by the name of Landour at the site of the present-day cantonment:

> Mussooree, the site of a station which is now one of the chief resorts of the visitors from the plains, stands at an elevation of seven thousand five hundred feet above the level of the sea, and is situated on the southern face of the ridge, called the Landour Range, and overlooking the village of that name, which has been chosen for the establishment of a military depot, or sanitorium [sic]…[56]

---

[53]Mundy G.C., *Pen and Pencil Sketches being the Journal of a Tour in India: Vol. I* (London: John Murray, Albemarle-Street, 1858), 188.

[54]Bodycot F., *Guide to Mussoorie* (Mussoorie: Mafasilite Printing Works, 1907), 68.

[55]White G.F., *Views in India–Chiefly Among the Himalaya Mountains* (London and Paris: Fisher Son & Co., 1838), 32.

[56]Ibid.

I would personally tend to concur with this explanation that Landour has been named after a village, which gave way to the cantonment. Although I cannot still say with certainty how Landour got its name. Anyway, as William Shakespeare said, 'What's in a name?'

Early Settlement

Mussoorie and Landour evolved as two separate townships[57], with Landour being a cantonment and Mussoorie a civil station.

Captain Young's residence, called 'Mullingar', was the first building to come up at Landour in 1826.[58] An Irishman himself, Young is believed to have named his house after a townland[59] named Mullingar in his home county of Donegal in Ireland. This townland is about two hours' drive from Young's hometown of Culdaff. Young had a close connection with Mullingar because Young's family owned properties in this townland in the nineteenth century.

Most often it is believed that Young's house was named after the town of Mullingar, which is the county town of County Westmeath, which is not true.

The founding father of Mussoorie is also believed to have arranged potato seeds from Ireland and is credited with planting the first potatoes in the Himalayas. His potato farm was located just below his house, owing to which Mullingar was also nicknamed 'The Potato Garden' and sometimes as 'Mulliagoes'.[60]

---

[57]Bodycot F., *Guide to Mussoorie* (Mussoorie: Mafasilite Printing Works, 1907), 64.
[58]Apart from Mullingar House there was also another building called Mullingar Cottage built on the same estate by Captain Young.
[59]A term used in Ireland and Scotland for a small territorial division of land, generally between 50 and 200 ha.
[60]Magowan R., 'From Donegal to Dehradun—Following Frederick Young's Footsteps' (2021). (An unpublished article written by a descendant of General

Young's house has withstood the ravages of time for nearly two centuries and still stands tall. Several families, many of them Tibetan, have snugly settled in this grand mansion.

After building his home at Landour, Young is said to have impressed upon Sir Charles Metcalfe—a British colonial administrator—who was on a visit to Mussoorie to establish a sanatorium for ailing soldiers at Landour.

In December 1827, Captain R. McMullen came up and started the task of building a hospital and barracks[61] for the 'Convalescent Depot' or sanatorium for ailing soldiers (referred to as the 'invalids') on top of the Landour hill. Although small groups of ailing soldiers arrived in 1828 and stayed in makeshift accommodations at Landour, the hospital and barracks were made functional from April 1829.

This infirmary gained rapid popularity as soldiers and officers—some sick and some feigning sickness to escape from the heat of the plains—arrived here in large numbers, and a few years later, this paved the way for the establishment of an army cantonment here.

> **Does Young still long for his mountain home?**
>
> Legends abound wherein residents claim sighting the legendary Captain (turned General) in the dark of the night. It is claimed that Young was seen riding a white horse in the compound of Mullingar. There are others who claim to have seen a parade of 'gora' soldiers in the compound, with Young in command. Perhaps the Irish soldier still longs for his home in the mountains!

Landour Bazaar

With the establishment of the Convalescent Depot at Landour, supplies were the need of the hour. The British, led by Captain

---

Frederick Young—which she kindly shared with the me.)

[61]The Rambler, *A Mussoorie Miscellany* (Mussoorie: Mafasilite Press, 1936), 14.

Young, encouraged merchants to come up from the plains and open establishments in Landour. A narrow stretch from the present-day clock tower, up to the ascent of the slope that leads to Mullingar (known as 'Mullingar slope'), was earmarked for the market. Seizing this opportunity, Indian entrepreneurs came rushing in from plains—ranging from towns in present-day Uttar Pradesh to Haryana.

A 1923 postcard showing the Landour Bazaar near the present-day clock tower. Noticeable are the shops owned by Indian merchants and the castle like structure seen in the centre is the gate to Castle Hill Estate. (Publisher: Raphael Tuck and Sons; Picture courtesy: Hotel Savoy, Mussoorie)

Soon enough, Landour became a flourishing market—the first market in Mussoorie. It was regarded among the most well-supplied markets of India with merchants sourcing their goods from England, France, America and other countries to cater to the requirements of the European population of Landour and Mussoorie.[62] The Landour

---

[62]Northam J., *Guide to Masuri, Landaur, Dehradun and The Hills North of Dehra* (Calcutta: Thacker, Spink and Co., 1884), 61.

merchants sold everything from jewellery and clothes to fruits and vegetables, groceries, sweets and grains.

In her diary,[63] Robert Moss King, who had visited Landour in 1878, commented about the shops in Landour: 'They all have their names in English over their shops and some are very comical. "Jugoo, Eggsman", "Kasi Nath, Dressmaker of Gents and Ladies", "Jalaloodeen, Moderate Price Shop", "Ram Lall, Shopkeeper", "Yusuf Mohammud, Sweets and Jams".'

There were also tailors and cobblers who catered to Europeans. Two banks and several moneylenders (mahajans) were forever in readiness to loan large and small amounts to the spendthrift gentry.

Another view of Landour Market sometime in the 1930s. (Picture courtesy: Hotel Savoy, Mussoorie)

By 1884 it is reported that there were more than 240 shops and houses in Landour Market.[64] In fact, there were shops along the

---

[63]King R.M., *The Diary of a Civilians Wife in India: 1877–1882; Vol. I* (London: Richard Bentley and Sons, 1884), 149–150.

[64]Northam J., *Guide to Masuri, Landaur, Dehradun and The Hills North of Dehra* (Calcutta: Thacker, Spink and Co., 1884), 61.

road, while the residences of Indian merchants were either on the lower ground floors or on the first floor. Most of the shops and residences are in a derelict condition today and were declared dangerous for habitation by the state government about a decade ago. But people still continue to live here.

In 1827, a post office was opened at Landour that was later shifted to Mussoorie in 1909, but a sub-post office is still functional at Landour Market (see chapter 15).

The Koh-i-Noor building in Landour, which was constructed around 1890 by an Indian family. Its twin turrets surmounted by metal crowns, stained-glass windows and ornately carved cast-iron lattices over the windows made it the most magnificent building in Landour. (Picture courtesy: Hotel Savoy, Mussoorie)

Landour also housed 'Nautch girls',[65] most of whom lived at Rajmandi—behind the bazaar towards the east. There was a

---

[65]The term 'nautch' is derived from the Urdu word 'naach', which means dance. Nautch was a popular dance performed by girls in the palaces of rajas and nawabs. The girls who performed were known as nautch girls.

building in Landour known as the 'Nautch ghar' where many of the girls stayed and also performed. Quite frequently, they were also invited for performances by rajas and maharajas to their palaces and bungalows in Mussoorie.

In the middle of the bazaar, just opposite the shops, is a yellow and white masonry structure—designed like the gate of a castle. This gate is the entrance to Castle Hill Estate, which is wrongly believed to be the residence of Prince Duleep Singh during his stay at Mussoorie. This property was originally owned by George Bladen Taylor who levelled a part of the property to create a playing field—known as The Taylor's Flat—which was used for hosting local cricket tournaments. This 182-acre property was purchased by the government for ₹3 lakhs for establishing the Survey of India offices here. In the early 1990s, survey offices were shifted, and the property now lies in a derelict state.

Further ahead, European residences commenced from the Mullingar slope with those on the slope fetching moderate rentals compared to those further up the hill.[66]

Char Dukan

As one reaches Mullingar Building, there is a fork in the road, and a left turn takes one towards Lal Tibba. Just before Lal Tibba is St. Peter's Church (see chapter 6), and this locality is known as Char Dukan. Why Char Dukan? Simple answer, there used to be four (char) shops here—although now the number is five.

'Mustn't the name be changed to "paanch dukan" now!' exclaimed a dear friend while we were sitting and enjoying 'cheese-maggi' at Vipin's shop at Char Dukan. Point to ponder.

The shops at Char Dukan are famous for Maggi noodles, omelettes, pancakes and waffles. Hundreds of tourists throng these

---

[66]Northam J., *Guide to Masuri, Landaur, Dehradun and The Hills North of Dehra* (Calcutta: Thacker, Spink and Co., 1884), 61.

A 1904 postcard showing the bridge at Char Dukan in Landour. This wooden bridge has since been cemented and made motorable. (Photographer: T.A. Rust)

eating joints, and the popularity of this place has increased over the past decade—ever since the master blaster Sachin Tendulkar became a visitor here for few years in a row, staying at his friend's house near Char Dukan. I do have a picture of him playing gully cricket at night with young boys at Char Dukan.

Just beyond Char Dukan, one has to crane one's neck to see the top of a high hill that lies beyond. This hill is called Lal Tibba ('Lal' meaning red and 'Tibba' meaning hill); perhaps, in the past, lot of rhododendron trees flourishing here, with their bright red flowers, earned this hill the name. Lal Tibba is the highest point of Mussoorie, and the Convalescent Depot was established on top of this hill. This area has been taken over by the DRDO[67]—I am sure such peaceful environs would help DRDO scientists in crafting new innovations for national security!

There is a deep gorge just beyond Char Dukan that, in the nineteenth century, was made passable by erecting a wooden bridge. A strong concrete structure has now replaced the wooden bridge.

---

[67]Defence Research and Development Organisation.

The Mall

Very few know that Landour too had a Mall Road! The Mall Road was more or less a level road that commenced from the 'wooden bridge' and continued towards the gate of Childer's Lodge, where the road turns towards the northwest face of Lal Tibba and passes between the Landour and Roman Catholic cemeteries (and a few houses above and below the road) to reach the Language School or the Kellogg's Church.[68] Here this road merges with another road coming up from Char Dukan.

Mall Road is today referred to as the Circular Road or 'Chakkar ki sadak', since a sharp right from Kellogg's Church leads one to the Landour Theatre (it was shut down decades ago) where theatrical events were held,[69] and then down to Char Dukan—completing a full round or a chakkar.

A left from Kellogg's and the road goes up towards 'The Sisters'. The Sisters was the place where the sisters, working at the Convalescent Depot, had their residences. Over the years a few shops came up near The Sisters and the place is now called The Sisters' Bazaar.

Beyond The Sisters are more bungalows, and then one can go down the crest to reach Tehri Road.

A military cantonment at Landour was established in 1872, spread over 1,070 acres with 80 private houses and 25 government bungalows that were residences for officers, and barracks for soldiers in addition to the hospital. In 1897, the military authorities got the Mussoorie Municipality to take over Landour Bazaar so now the boundary of Landour Cantonment commences from the slope of Mullingar Hill. The present area of the cantonment is 718 acres.

---

[68]Kinney T., *The Echo Guide to Mussoorie* (Mussoorie: Echo Press, 1908), 40.

[69]Hawthorne R. *The Beacon's Guide to Mussoorie* (Mussoorie: The Beacon Press, 1890), 31.

An 1880s picture of a theatrical group at Landour. (Picture courtesy: Hotel Savoy, Mussoorie)

Today, Landour Cantonment is the most sought-after address in Mussoorie, and a house at Landour is worth millions. It is the residence of who's who of the country, which include the celebrated author Ruskin Bond, who lives at Ivy Cottage. Bond's neighbour is Bollywood director Vishal Bhardwaj. Noted actor Victor Banerjee's house is called the Parsonage, which is located on the Mall Road or Circular Road. Author and historian Ganesh Saili resides at the Trim Lodge near Mullingar Building. Journalist and former co-owner of NDTV Prannoy Roy's summer abode is Bellevue, near The Sisters. The Alter brothers, Tom[70]—the Bollywood actor—and Steve—a noted author—live at Oakville, which is just outside the cantonment boundary.

---

[70]Tom Alter passed away on 29 September 2017.

The Clock Tower

The saga of Landour is incomplete without any mention of the clock tower, which has a close emotional connection with the residents of Landour.

The clock tower was 'first' constructed by the Mussoorie Municipality in 1938-1939. For the residents of Landour, the clock tower was their address. 'Just write my name followed by "Clock Tower, Mussoorie" and the letter will reach me,' any resident would say.

The old clock tower of Landour that was constructed in 1938–1939 and demolished in 2010.

Around 2009, seventy years after it was constructed, there were reports that the structure of the tower had weakened. In March 2010, the municipal authorities decided to demolish the allegedly 'weakened' tower, amidst protests by citizens.

A few months later, in September, I got a call early in the morning from Mr Bhandari, a Mussoorie resident. 'Mr Tom Alter

Bollywood actor and Mussoorie resident, the late Tom Alter sitting on a 'silent protest' against the demolition of the clock tower of Landour in 2010.

is sitting on a "maun vrat" (a vow of silence) at clock tower. He has asked me to inform you. Please join,' Bhandari said.

I dressed up hurriedly and reached Landour to find Mr Alter and a few residents sitting on the roadside near the demolished clock tower. A picture of the clock tower was kept in front of them.

'What is the purpose of your maun vrat, sir?' I enquired.

'This is to remember an old friend who is gone forever,' Mr Alter wrote on a piece of paper. 'I am observing silence for twelve hours to pay homage to the demolished clock tower,' the great man added.

I also sat alongside him and other citizens. After a while, he passed me another piece of paper that expressed his memories

of the old clock tower: 'Its echo was music far and near;
It heralded the night, it brought the morning near.'

The result of this 'silent protest' was that within five days, the municipal officials laid the foundation stone for a new tower, although it took more than five years for it to be completed.

At night, the chimes of the new clock tower can be heard at my house, reminding me of Mr Alter's words: 'Its echo was music far and near!'

Pari Tibba

Are paris (fairies) for real? Do they possess supernatural powers? Do they frequent terrestrial places? These and so many more questions come to mind whenever there is a discussion regarding Pari Tibba. Believe me, dear readers, Pari Tibba is shrouded in mystery.

Pari Tibba is a hill behind the students' hostel of Woodstock School, which is believed to be frequented by 'paris'. Local residents—senior citizens and youngsters alike—swear on God that fairies visit this hill. The myths and stories surrounding Pari Tibba are more bizarre than any of the European ghost tales that I have shared in various chapters of this book. Tales about Pari Tibba have also been documented in guide books of Mussoorie.

The Rambler (1936)[71] mentions that Pari Tibba is also known as 'Burnt Hill' or 'Witch's Hill'. He mentions old ruins on top of this hill and says that according to locals, old buildings were reduced to ruins by djinns or paris.

Intrigued by the mystery surrounding this hill, I made a visit. I found that the hilltop was absolutely barren and devoid of any trees. There were some old ruins on the top, while at one point there were also some strange stones assembled together; it seemed as if someone had put a red tika on these stones, and some dried flowers were also lying about.

---

[71]The Rambler, *A Mussoorie Miscellany* (Mussoorie: Mafasilite Press, 1936), 10.

'This is an ancient temple, a temple where paris come and pray,' said Sawan, who lived nearby and had accompanied me to Pari Tibba.

'And what about the tika and flowers, were these offered by the paris?' I enquired.

'No, no,' he exclaimed. 'Sometimes residents of Dhobighat come here to pray in these temples. These must've been left by them.'

Apart from the old ruins, it seemed that an attempt had been recently made to construct a building towards the southern end of the hilltop.

'About ten years ago, a businessman from Delhi attempted to build a resort here, but it was never completed. At night, the paris would demolish the walls until the businessman gave up,' Sawan told me.

'What rubbish! Must be some locals who do not want any construction here,' I mocked in an attempt to provoke Sawan.

'Sir, you people never seem to understand. The owner of this place also thought the same and deployed several guards to catch the culprit, but a few hours past midnight, all the guards would fall asleep and, in the morning, the walls would be razed to the ground,' Sawan retorted, sounding a bit offended.

I spoke to several residents, particularly those living near Dhobighat, and I was told that in the past this hill had frequently been struck by lightning and that had given this hill a black, charred appearance and hence, the British named it the 'Burnt Hill'.

I came across another interesting mention by The Rambler (1936)[72] that referred to a horrifying incident that occurred at Pari Tibba. He narrates an incident involving a young girl and a young man in the British army. The girl's father became indebted to a merchant and was forced to give his daughter in marriage to the ageing merchant—much against the wishes of the young girl. Few years later, the young girl—who had since become a mother—fell

---

[72]Ibid, 11.

ill and was forced to come back to Mussoorie to recuperate. As luck would have it, her young lover (now a Captain) was also at Mussoorie on 'furlough', and cupid struck again!

The girl's husband, who lived in the plains, was furious when he came to know about his wife's affair and planned to take action against the couple. Somehow, the lovers came to know about the approaching danger. Although it was late in the evening, the loving couple decided to elope and take the goat tracks to Dehradun. As they descended from Landour Ridge and reached the vicinity of Pari Tibba, it started raining, and so they decided to take shelter in the ruins. But lightning stuck the ruins, bringing an end to their unhappy lives!

The couple was believed to have been buried at Pari Tibba, and The Rambler also mentions that a small structure to the north of the ruins seemed to be the final resting place of the lovers. Unfortunately, I could not locate this structure.

To me, Pari Tibba or the Burnt Hill remains the most mysterious place within the Mussoorie and Landour landscapes!

3

THE MAKING OF A HILL STATION

The British had taken a fancy to the idyllic mountainside, stunning vistas and pleasing weather (at least during the summers) of Mussoorie, so much so that during the 1850s and early 1860s there were speculations that the town may even become the 'summer capital' of the Raj. But residents were soon left heartbroken as this distinction was conferred on Shimla (then Simla) in 1864.

The rivalry between Shimla and Mussoorie continues as residents of both these hill stations stake claim upon the title of 'Queen of the Hills', and being a Mussoorie resident, I reiterate that my town has indisputable and unequivocal claim over this tag. Speaking about this age-old rivalry between the two hill towns, I also take pride in informing the readers that Mussoorie formed a municipal committee (for details, see chapter 1) nine years before Shimla!

The Raj-era Mussoorie Municipal Committee (or Municipal Board, as it was later reconstituted) was reported to be highly efficient. The development of civic amenities, including roads, water supply and sewerage, was taken up at a rapid pace. Street lights were introduced using gas lamps, and later, the Municipal Board also facilitated the electrification of the town. Let us trace Mussoorie's development during the nineteenth and twentieth centuries.

The Journey to Mussoorie

For those enamoured by the charm of the Queen of the Hills, looking to escape the sultry heat of Indian plains, the journey to the 'mountain heaven' was by no means easy.

In old journals and travelogues, writers often lament the long and tiresome journey from the plains to reach the Queen of the Hills during the nineteenth century. Saharanpur (or Saharanpore, as the goras called it) was the place from whence one embarked upon the journey to Mussoorie—a two-day ordeal according to various old accounts. None too comfortable dak garhis,[73] starting from Saharanpur in the wee hours of the morning, took the better part of the day to cover the 70-odd kilometres to Rajpur. The more daring travellers would choose the night garhis to reach Dehradun by early morning.

An 1884 advertisement of Messrs Buckle and Co., who ran dak garhis between Saharanpur and Rajpur and also supplied jhampans, dandys and horses for the journey between Rajpur and Mussoorie. This company also transported freight between Mussoorie and Saharanpur. (Source: Bodycot F., Guide to Mussoorie, Mussoorie: Mafasilite Printing Works, 1907)

---

[73]A carriage, driven by horses, that was in operation during the nineteenth and early part of twentieth centuries for carrying post (dak). This carriage also had room for a few passengers.

Passing through densely forested Siwaliks, many travellers were rudely woken from their slumber when their carriage abruptly stopped to give the right of way to a herd of elephants; or when they were jostled by frantic shouts of '*Sher! Sher!*' by the coachman, as a tiger lurking in the dense undergrowth was sighted. As the coach would resume its journey, such encounters would force a prayer upon the lips of even the most fervent atheists.

As a precaution, many coachmen would also keep fireworks in order to scare away the wild animals: 'Even with those precautions, no fool insurance company would have given you a life policy for there was always danger of meeting a mast elephant, which no amount of rockets or fireworks would deter from charging if it wants to, for it simply must,' observes Williams (1936).[74]

Williams also mentions a certain Mr Carter—who was killed by shock when a tiger attacked his dak garhi.[75]

In her journal, Lady Dufferin[76] recounts shooting down three big cats in a single day in these forests—no wonder only a handful of tigers were left in India by the time the inveterate 'shikari sahebs' were done with their hunting. Thankfully, this area is a national park today, spanning over 820 km².

A famine at Dehradun, in 1861, and the need for food supplies prompted the government to construct a road through the Siwaliks, and also the tunnel near Asarodi. This made the commute between Saharanpur and Dehradun a bit easier as it later enabled bus travel between the two stations.

---

[74]The Rambler, *A Mussoorie Miscellany* (Mussoorie: Mafasilite Press, 1936), 50.
[75]Ibid.
[76]Lady Dufferin was the wife of the Viceroy and Governor-General (1884–1888). She describes her visits to Doon in 1885 and 1887 in her journals. Marchioness of Dufferin and Ava, *Our Viceregal Life in India: Vol. II* (London: John Murray, 1890), 151.

A few years ago, the authorities managed to put a dandi on display on the Mall Road near Jhoola Ghar. How they managed to acquire the dandi is a tale on its own.

A friend of mine, Mr S.M. Sharma—posted in Mussoorie with the local development authority—who has a keen interest in the town's history, once shared his idea of putting a dandi on public display.

'Brilliant!' I said. 'I will pen down a few words about the history of dandi and you can put a label alongside the dandi,' I suggested.

'But without the dandi, will this label be of any use?' he questioned and explained that frantic searches for a dandi with all kabaadi-wallahs and antique dealers in Mussoorie and Doon had yielded no result.

'We came to know that the Maharaja of Kapurthala owns a fine dandi, but he is not willing to part with his prized family possession,' Mr Sharma lamented.

I remembered my grandfather had once mentioned that he had bought a dandi for my grandmother. Is it still lying somewhere in the godown in the basement of my brother's office? I thought.

Next morning, I hired a few Nepali labourers and started the onerous task of 'unearthing' the dandi in the huge godown that is still flush with all kinds of furniture and stuff.

To cut the story short, the dandi was found in the godown and given to the authorities. It is on display near Jhoolaghar with my epithet!

The opening of a rail route between Haridwar and Dehradun in 1900 was a watershed moment in the history of travel to Doon and Mussoorie, and it reduced the dependence upon the old route through Saharanpur.[77]

Upon reaching Rajpur, after a nights' rest, the weary traveller embarked upon the seven-mile (about 11 kilometres) journey to Mussoorie via Rajpur. Horses were hired at Rajpur for the uphill climb, while men and women unaccustomed to riding chose a

---

[77]The Rambler, *A Mussoorie Miscellany* (Mussoorie: Mafasilite Press, 1936), 56.

dandi[78] or a jhampan,[79] which were carried by a team of four to eight porters. The sick and the elderly also invariably choose the latter options. In the later years, a kandi[80] was also added to the repertoire of the porters for carrying children.

At a toll-booth just beyond Rajpur, visitors had to pay a tax for their entourage in order to enter 'the gates of paradise'.

At the foot of Rajpore. - Showing part of Mussoorie Hill.

Rajpur in the early twentieth century. Noticeable are the bullock carts on the side of the street.

---

[78]A dandi resembled a canoe-shaped structure with horizontal poles at both ends. The wooden frame of the dandi was covered with a thick cloth or tarpaulin. Passengers would sit inside the dandi while porters would carry it on their shoulders through the projecting poles at the front and back.

[79]A jhampan resembled a chair with long horizontal poles projecting from the corners in the front as well as the rear. Four porters—two at the back and two at the front—carried the poles on their shoulders. The jhampan was covered by a canopy of tarpaulin or oil cloth.

[80]A kandi was a small basket made of cane. Children sat in the kandi, which was carried like a backpack by the porters.

Rates of toll tax at Rajpur (sometime in 1880s)

Porter	1 paisa
Jhampan	8 annas (50 paisa)
Dandi	4 annas (25 paisa)
Horse	4 annas (25 paisa)
Pony	2 annas (12.5 paisa)

A steep climb over a narrow, meandering road cut into the mountainside was taxing on both the rider and the horse while sapping the energy of even the ostensibly indefatigable porters used to these slopes. The sideward rocking of dandis and jhampans often forced a stifled cry from the passengers.

The steep climb from Rajpur to Mussoorie. Seen in this picture are porters carrying heavy luggage as well as a few men carrying a jhampan.

About half-way to Mussoorie, at Jharipani, the travellers would stop for much-needed refreshments at a café appropriately christened as 'Half-Way House'! '...where the thirsty traveller might refresh himself by a brandy or whisky peg, a small bottle of claret or a cup of tea,' observes John Northam.[81]

The Half-Way House at Jharipani, which offered refreshment and retiring rooms to the travellers. This building still exists albeit in a dilapidated condition. A board of Crown Brewery can be seen at the entrance. (Picture courtesy: Hotel Savoy, Mussoorie)

The horses and porters also took a well-deserved break before toiling on. A crumbling and uninhabited building is what remains now of the once sought-after Half-Way House.

After crossing Jharipani comes Barlowganj, from where one road led to Gandhi Chowk and another, albeit a much steeper one, towards Masonic Lodge and Landour. Both these roads are motorable today.

---

[81]Northam J., *Guide to Masuri, Landaur, Dehradun and the Hills North of Dehra* (Calcutta: Thacker, Spink and Co., 1884), 29.

The road from Barlowganj towards Mussoorie in the early twentieth century.

Meanwhile, in the formative years of this town, the connecting roads between Mussoorie and Landour—including the Mall Road—were narrow hill tracks scooped out of the hillside, dangerously perched over the edge of steep precipices, which were causing frequent accidents, especially for horse riders—many of whom fell to their deaths in the deep ravines, while a lucky few were able to desperately cling to projecting rocks or trees, clamouring for help. The earliest accidents of riders include that of a Major Blundell and also of a Private in the Scottish rifles—both fell down steep precipices in Landour.[82]

A couple met their maker at Camel's Back Road when a kastura[83] bird startled the horse of the lady, and as the gentleman tried to grab the bridle of the lady's pony, both the horses bolted and the couple and their mounts were hurled down the gorge.[84]

'Mr T. of the artillery met with a serious accident this morning.

---

[82]The Rambler, *A Mussoorie Miscellany* (Mussoorie: Mafasilite Press, 1936), 65–66.
[83]Himalayan Whistling Thrush.
[84]The Rambler, *A Mussoorie Miscellany* (Mussoorie: Mafasilite Press, 1936), 66.

The road was much broken and as he attempted to ride over it, it gave way; he and his pony went down the precipice. Mr T. was stopped in his descent, after he had gone one hundred feet, by a tree, was brought up and carried to a surgeon [...] but is expected to recover [...] The pony went down 250 feet, and was found alive!' writes Fanny Parks,[85] the wife of a British civil servant, in her travelogue. The municipal body put all its resources on the development of roads, starting from around late 1840s, and by the 1880s, significant progress had been made. A major stretch of the 2-kilometre-long Mall Road was laid, and by mid-1880s, the steep and dangerous incline towards Landour was also widened, providing a safe passage to those used to riding from Landour to the Mall during the evenings and mornings.

View from Library Verandah, looking E. — Mussoori

The hand-pulled rickshaws that were a popular mode of transport on Mall Road until the mid-1990s when the Lal Bahadur Shastri National Academy of Administration (LBSNAA) initiated the transformation of hand-pulled rickshaws into cycle rickshaws to spare the rickshaw pullers the agony of pushing and pulling the rickshaws up and down the hill.

[85]Parks F., *Wanderings of a Pilgrim, in Search of the Picturesque: During Four-and-Twenty Years in the East* (London: Pelham Richardson, 1850), 248–249.

The local ponies, tormented by many a scared rider who clung tightly to the bridles for dear life, must have also got a breather.

From Bullock Carts to Cars

While the travellers seemed quite content with the seven-mile horse ride, trek or being lifted on jhampans, getting supplies to the 6,000-feet-high hill station was a daunting task. Nevertheless, the multitude of untiring porters toiled up and down the hillside, carrying all and sundry—from a case of wine to even a piano!

'As you go slowly along, you overtake battalions of coolies, with burdens on their heads…'[86]

But budding local businesses were none too happy about porters gobbling up their profits—also frequently grumbling about delays in supplies.

It was Mackinnon (a leading businessman) who came to the rescue. A joint stock company was formed to carve a road out of the hillside to enable freight 'carts' to trudge up the hill. Businessmen were eager to chip in, and soon ₹60,000 was raised.

Work started around 1843, with Mackinnon taking the lead in designing and constructing this road—which came to be known as 'Mackinnon's Road'[87] or years later as 'Mackinnon's Cart Road'. The road traversed a distance of around 14 miles (22 kilometres) to connect Rajpur with Gandhi Chowk.

It took over a century to develop Mackinnon's picturesque, winding road into a motorable one. However, nothing was going to deter Colonel E.W. Bell[88] from driving a motorcar on this narrow cart track. In 1920, Bell drove a Ford car from Rajpur to

---

[86]Northam J., *Guide to Masuri, Landaur, Dehradun and the Hills North of Dehra* (Calcutta: Thacker, Spink and Co., 1884), 26.

[87]Ibid, 24.

[88]Colonel Bell was the son-in-law of the Swetenhams who owned the Cloud's End Estate. He was also the municipal engineer (see chapter 4).

Mussoorie and reached the Mall—although it took another three decades for another driver to emulate him!

A government loan enabled the Municipal Board to develop 'Mackinnon's Cart Road' into a motorable road up to Bhatta village in 1927. By 1930, it was further extended to within 4 kilometres from Mussoorie and, in 1936, up to Kincraig—which became a major bus terminus.[89]

> The Gwalior and Northern India Transport (GNIT) Co. Ltd—a company owned by the Scindia's of Gwalior—ran buses between Saharanpur and Mussoorie. GNIT also had the contract for carrying Royal Mail on this route.
>
> Abundance of nails and horseshoes on the road—left by the passing bullocks or horses—caused frequent punctures to bus tyres. The problem was resolved by getting people on contract to regularly scout the road and remove the annoying metals.[90]
>
> There's another interesting bit of history: since the 1930s, this company, owned by Jiwaji Rao Scindia—the Maharaja of Gwalior—was also plying buses in Delhi.
>
> In May 1948, the Centre took over the Scindia's bus company and renamed it the Delhi Transport Service—later to be christened as the Delhi Transport Corporation in 1971.

A motorable road up to Gandhi Chowk was built in 1954 and subsequently, in 1957, a motor road was built up to the Masonic Lodge.

For some strange reason, Mackinnon's Cart Road—which is now a busy highway—is known today as the 'Cart McKenzie' Road.

'We never had any McKenzie in Mussoorie! Did we?' Mr Hugh Gantzer called to enquire one morning. While I have been unable to find a Mr McKenzie, I am still trying to figure out why and how the name of this road was changed.

---

[89]Hari Har Lal P., *The Doon Valley Down the Ages* (New Delhi: Interprint, 1993), 223.

[90]Ibid.

The First Spark

By 1875, the town was lit up with street lights, fuelled by carbide, on acetylene lamps that were called 'roorkee' (or 'rurki') lamp posts—perhaps the lamps were made in the town of Roorkee and hence the name. This 'shining example' even prompted the Lucknow Municipality to consider sending a deputation to study the street lights of Mussoorie.[91]

The growing population also necessitated the need for water supply and sewerage. The municipality took up the task of setting up a sewerage system, starting from the late 1800s, which is still functional—although over the past decade, the present government has spent crores over a new sewerage system, which is not yet fully operational.

Springs located on either side of the town were tapped and their water pumped up the slopes to storage tanks located on high ridges. Initially, about three springs were tapped; heavy duty pumps were imported from Germany and the United Kingdom, and these were run with generators—many of these pumps are still functional!

The water supply soon proved inadequate as more and more people flocked to the picturesque hill station. A hydro-power project at nearby Kempty Falls (under territory of Tehri kingdom) was planned to provide electricity for driving the pumps and also for lighting the twin towns of Mussoorie and Landour. This ambitious plan fell flat as the ruler of Tehri did not permit the British to set up the project in his territory.[92]

Bhatta Falls, located on the southern face of the ridge towards Dehradun, emerged as a viable alternative. The power plant was set up at Galogi, in a deep gorge alongside the Bhatta stream, with an outlay of ₹11.50 lakhs, and with a capacity of 750 KW

---

[91]Bodycot F., *Guide to Mussoorie* (Mussoorie: Mafasilite Printing Works, 1907), 9.
[92]Government of United Provinces, *Completion Report of the Mussoorie Hydro-Electric Scheme, Vol. I.* (Allahabad: Government Press, United Province, 1914), 2.

(enhanced to 3 MW in the present day).

Visitors can locate this spot after going about one and a half kilometres towards Mussoorie from the check post at Kolhukhet. A small tin-shed on the roadside, overlooking a deep gorge, marks the spot. A careful peek down the gorge reveals the power plant about 500 metres below the road.

The cable-car at Galogi

For ferrying supplies and officials to the Galogi power station, a cable-car was installed. This cable-car was shut down several decades ago after a motorable road to Galogi was constructed. Noted travel writer and a distinguished resident, Mr Hugh Gantzer, recalls travelling in the cable-car that went down the steep precipice to the station.

'I am perhaps the only person alive who had taken the cable-car to the power station. It was some journey!' Mr Gantzer recalls.

He trudged along with his father Mr. J.F. Gantzer, the then Chairman of Mussoorie Municipal Board, on a visit to the station. Few officials of the municipal board also formed a part of the entourage.

The cable-car had a fenced platform at the front, on which sat a signalman with a red and a green flag for signalling the operator sitting down below to start or stop.

'Upon reaching midway down the cliff, my father found the view of the Bhatta stream and surroundings to be perfect for a photograph and asked for [the] cable-car to be stopped,' he recalls. 'Panic gripped an officer when a strong wind caused the car to violently rock to-and-fro while it was hanging several hundred feet above the ground.'

'"Wave the green flag! Wave the green flag! Take us down," shouted the panicked officer. The signalman merely smiled at the predicament of the officer and looked at my father who reluctantly nodded,' tells Mr Gantzer.

Once the cable-car reached the station, the shaken officer was the first to jump off.

'I swear to God, I will never again set a foot in this damned cable-car!' he announced before storming off.

Later, a motorable road to the station was developed and the cable-car was discontinued (a tin-shed at the roadside still marks the cable-car station).

Galogi, India's second hydro-power plant, was operationalized in 1909. 24 May 1909—the day Mussoorie was electrified—was chosen as it was 'Empire Day'—the birth anniversary of Queen Victoria, who had died in 1901.

The Criterion, Mussoorie.

A postcard from 1910. Seen in the centre is the electric pole outside the Mussoorie Library building (present-day Gandhi Chowk) on which the first electric bulb was lit up in 1909. Criterion Restaurant is visible in the background.

On the evening of this momentous day, as the first electric bulb lit up in Mussoorie, the quiet hill station, nestled in the hills of Uttarakhand, became one of the first towns in the country to get electricity. British citizens assembled under a utility pole at Gandhi Chowk and sang their royal anthem, 'God Save the Queen', while many were perplexed, scared and in awe of the never-before-seen bright lights.

The historic pole, which heralded the advent of electricity, was dismantled a few years ago, and has been relocated to the Municipal Garden. I went to the Municipal Garden to have a look at the pole, which I found was made by 'J&A Law Ironfounders' from Glasgow.

The electric pole exists even today, although it has been shifted to the Municipal Gardens. Residents as well as tourists are quite oblivious to the history of this pole.

Meanwhile, back in 1909, with rumours rife that electricity may harm humans, the municipal officials had a hard time convincing residents to get a power connection. Rummaging through old records, Gopal Bhardwaj, a resident historian, informs me that the ever-adventurous Colonel E.W. Bell[93] (civil and electrical engineer of municipality) went on to wrap electrical wires and hold the bulb close to his body to prove that it was safe to get bulbs installed.

For several years, electric lights in Mussoorie 'winked' every evening! No, I am not speaking about any supernatural occurrence; rather, the authorities dimmed them for three minutes at 9 p.m., which was called 'winking'—some believe this was done to indicate the time. This practice was discontinued in 1934 as it was found to be in violation of government norms.

Later on, Galogi also supplied electricity to parts of Doon, and is currently in operation and providing supply to Jharipani and Barlowganj localities of Mussoorie.

The Elusive Railway

The railway connecting Dehradun to Haridwar and beyond was opened for traffic on 1 March 1900, enabling the gentry to take this route and escape the agony of dak garhis from Saharanpur.

---

[93]The same gentleman who had driven a car from Rajpur to Mussoorie way back in 1920.

By this time, Darjeeling[94] (1881) was already connected by a mono-rail, while work was well underway to connect Ooty[95] (1908) and Shimla[96] (1903).

Not to be left behind, there was a furore amongst the who's who of Mussoorie, and demands for a similar railway were raised. The Municipal Board is believed to have done some spadework in this regard, but nothing materialized owing to the paucity of funds and subsequent outbreak of World War I. Finally, headway was made in 1921. Belti Shah Gilani, a businessman, floated the 'Dehradun–Mussoorie Electric Tramway Company Ltd'.

Within a short time, a share capital of ₹36 lakh was raised by the company, with many an astute businessmen jumping upon this 'profitable' opportunity.

Most notable investor was Maharaja Ripudaman Singh of Nabha (Punjab) with an investment of a whooping ₹10 lakh. He was persuaded by his accountant general who 'took advantage of this investment by getting his semi-educated son a job in the tramway company'.[97]

'Only two hours from Dehradun to Mussoorie!' company officials proclaimed.

A station at Jharipani with the terminus at Hotel Himalaya Club at Landour were planned. Notified land (classified as forests) near Rajpur was denotified and placed under the Mussoorie

---

[94]Built between 1879 and 1881, this 88-kilometre-long railway from New Jalpaiguri to Darjeeling climbs to an elevation of 2,200 metres (7,218 feet) above sea level. In 1999, UNESCO declared it as a World Heritage Site.

[95]The planning for this railway was done in 1854, but construction was started in the 1890s. The railway was opened for traffic in June 1899, between Mettupalayam to Coonoor, and by 1908, this picturesque railway connected Ooty as well. It has been declared by UNESCO as a World Heritage Site in 2005.

[96]This famous 'toy train'—picturized in several Bollywood movies—was completed over a period of five years, starting from 1898.

[97]Hari Har Lal P., *The Doon Valley Down the Ages* (New Delhi: Interprint, 1993), 224.

Municipality[98] to enable the laying of tracks in this area.

Work was stalled when an under-construction tunnel (between Rajpur and Jharipani) caved in and a few workers were killed. Before work could restart, charges of misappropriation of funds were made against Belti Shah, and the ambitious railway project was derailed.

One of the tunnels built between Rajpur and Jharipani for the railway.

Legal proceedings were initiated against Belti Shah, who became 'Guilty Shah'—a name by which he is still referred by the octogenarians of the town.

The company went into liquidation and all investors suffered heavy losses. What remains today are rusty railway tracks and old crumbling tunnels—gloomy remnants of an elusive dream and of hopes and aspirations of old citizens of the 'Queen of the Hills'.

---

[98]Ibid.

4

THE FAR WEST

The British history of Mussoorie may go back just two centuries, but the landscape has always been the abode of Lord Balram, the elder brother of Lord Krishna, that is, if myths surrounding a white temple and the black stone statue inside it are to be believed. Devotees from far and wide visit the shrine of Balram, located on top of the Bhadraj Hill. It is still believed that Lord Balram fulfils all wishes of his devotees.

Legends and folklore abound about the arrival of Lord Balram or 'Balbhadra' to this land during the battle of Kurukshetra in the Mahabharata. It is said that Balram did not participate in this epic battle and retired to the hills, and reached Bhadraj peak—a high hill located about 15 kilometres to the west of Mussoorie, offering magnificent views of snow-capped Himalayas, as well as the Doon Valley.

He meditated atop the hill and interacted with local villagers—most of whom were rearing cows. He would occasionally help them out and teach them various nuances of hand-to-hand combat.

When it was time to leave, Balram had to promise the disconsolate villagers that he would return. This is what is said to have happened next:

> Many centuries after Lord Balram's departure, Nandu Mehra, a villager, was digging for taro[99] roots on the banks of river Yamuna. He was irritated as a large brown stone underneath the taro plant blocked his access to the roots. He dug deeper, but to his surprise, he found it was no mere stone, but an idol.

---

[99]*Colocasia esculenta*—the roots are used as a vegetable.

Forgetting about his quest for the taro root, Mehra focused on unearthing the idol, which he managed to dig out after considerable effort. An exhausted Mehra slumped on the ground, staring at the large idol lying on the ground beside him.

'Which God does it belong to?' he wondered. 'It is not a Shiva idol, nor does it seem to be a Vishnu idol. Which God is this? And how did this idol happen to be in this forest,' Mehra thought.

This is when he was startled by a loud voice that came out of nowhere.

'O good man, I am Lord Balbhadra. You must take my idol to the highest point and place it there,' it said.

Mehra jumped up and reached for the idol, when he realized something. 'It's so very large and heavy, Lord, how will I carry it up the hill?' he pleaded.

'Do not worry, you will be able to lift it easily. You can place it down whenever you find it heavy,' the booming voice told him.

Mehra gingerly tried to pick up the idol and, to his surprise, it was light as a feather! He ambled up the hillside, following divine direction. After some time, Mehra felt thirsty. He looked around, but there was no water to be found in the forest.

'Oh God, I am dying of thirst. Please help me!' he prayed.

He heard the divine voice again, directing him to go a little further and clear some stones and mud. 'You will get water to quench you thirst,' he was told.

Soon, Mehra unearthed a source of clear, refreshing water. This water source exists even today at Matongi village, near Bhadraj!

A little while later, Mehra reached the top of a high hill and, suddenly, found the idol becoming heavy, so heavy that he could no longer lift it and had to place it on the ground.

It is believed that since then, this hill has been known as Bhadraj, and Lord Balbhadra has been residing here since centuries.

As far back as 1838, British traveller Fanny Parks discovered the idol on a visit to Bhadraj and recorded that it was in a neglected state.

'A little further we found a Hindu idol, rudely cut in stone; this idol is now neglected but was formally much worshipped,' Parks wrote.[100]

The Bhadraj Temple during the monsoons. The rock in front of the temple is the Surveyor's Stone.

Today, there is a grand temple at Bhadraj, thronged by devotees, especially in August, when an annual temple fair is attended by thousands of devotees from far and wide. There is a belief that the wishes of the visitors to the temple are fulfilled.

---

[100]Parks F., *Wanderings of a Pilgrim in Search of the Picturesque: Vol. II* (London: Pelham Richardson, 1850), 247.

Surveyor's Stone

Now that we know people lived and thrived in the Mussoorie landscape far before the British 'discovered' it, let's get into which Britishers were the first to climb these hills.

The large inscriptions on a boulder just outside the Bhadraj Temple—John Anthony Hodgson'; 'JSB' (for John Stuart Boldero); 'WLG' (for William Linnaeus Gardner); and 'Lady Hood 1814—prove that Young and Shore were not the first Britishers to climb the hills of Mussoorie in 1823!

The Surveyor's Stone outside the Bhadraj Temple with 'Lady Hood 1814' etched on it. This relic is getting defaced by the tourists.

In his journal, Hodgson notes the height of Bhadraj as 7,320 feet. This rock was apparently a survey marker used for triangulation in the great trigonometric survey started in 1802 by Lieutenant Colonel William Lambton,[101] and later completed by Sir George

---

[101]Lambton was a British soldier and surveyor who started the survey of the

Everest. It is a common belief that the names chiselled on the rock are those of a party of surveyors who had reached Bhadraj in 1814.

I am of the firm opinion that John Anthony Hodgson[102] was the only person out of this coterie who actually visited Bhadraj in 1814. What about the other two names then?

An excerpt from Hodgson's journal, dated 29 March 1814, reads: 'I set out up the Valley for the Budrajh[103] Mountain, round which the Jumna flows into the Doon.'[104]

Another account from Hodgson's journal says: 'Climbed Bhadraj and other prominent hills; took obsns. to snowy peaks and sketched as much of the country as I could.'

There is no account of Hodgson being accompanied by any other notable companion. It seems that Hodgson got his name chiselled, along with 'WLG' referring to William Linnaeus Gardner,[105] his former boss. Gardner was the settlement officer for various districts in Haryana, and Hodgson had served under him earlier. No record of Gardner's visit to Bhadraj has been found. By etching Gardner's initials on the rock, perhaps Hodgson wanted to appease his former boss and a senior officer. Who knows!

As for Lady Hood[106], in an entry subsequent to his visit to Bhadraj, Hodgson's journal says, 'As I was re-entering our districts, I met with Lady Hood going into the Doon Valley, and, as it was

---

Indian peninsula from the east coast to the west coast. Sir George Everest took up the triangulation work after Lambton's death in 1823.

[102]Hodgson went on to become the Surveyor General of India in 1821.

[103]Read 'Bhadraj'

[104]Phillimore R.H., *Historical Records of Survey of India: Vol. II, 1800 to 1815* (Dehradun: Survey of India, 1950), 81.

[105]Gardner was a British soldier who raised the 2nd Lancers (Gardner's Horse) regiment for the British army in 1809. Prior to joining the British army, Gardner was in service of the Holkar's of Indore.

[106]Lady Hood held significant clout, too, as she was then the wife of Vice-admiral Sir Samuel Hood, who was in command of the British naval fleet in the East Indies. Her full name was Mary Elizabeth Frederica Mackenzie.

her Ladyship's wish, I thought it incumbent upon me to conduct her thro' the valley to Haridwar.'

There is no account of Lady Hood's visit to Bhadraj, although Hodgson does mention their visit to 'the hot springs at Sahasradhara'.

So perhaps the name of Lady Hood was etched on the rock subsequently—a fact corroborated by Fanny Parks, a traveller who visited Bhadraj in 1838. Parks observes:

> Near it is a large stone, on which is chiselled, "Lady Hood, 1814:" on speaking of this to the political agent, he laughed and said, "You were more enterprising than Lady Hood; you visited the spot,—she only sent a man to chisel out her name, and that of Colonel B—on the top of Bhadraj; she never visited the place in person."[107]

'Colonel B. would account for the inscription 'JSB' or John Stuart Boldero, who was then the Joint Magistrate of Saharanpur, another influential officer.

First British to Set Foot in Mussoorie Hills

While we have settled the mystery of the rock inscriptions, let me tell my readers that there are records of the British arriving at the Mussoorie Ridge even before 1814. Yes, even Hodgson (JSB) was not the first gora to climb up these hills.

The first British party to traverse these hills may have been an expedition group looking for the origin of the Ganges. Major James Rennell, Surveyor General of Bengal, who had set out to find the holy river's origin around 1764, believed that the Ganges originated from the Mansarovar Lake.[108] It was believed that a

---

[107]Parks F., *Wanderings of a Pilgrim in Search of the Picturesque: Vol. II* (London: Pelham Richardson, 1850), 248.

[108]Phillimore R.H., *Historical Records of Survey of India: Vol II, 1800 to 1815*

tunnel ran through the Himalayas, channelling the water from the holy lake to Gangotri, which was thought to be the mouth of this tunnel.[109]

In 1808, an exploration party—led by William Spencer Webb, along with Hyder Young Hearsey[110] and Felix Vincent Raper—started from Haridwar to Gangotri. This group was the first British party to scramble up the Mussoorie Ridge. They crossed the range towards the east of present-day Landour.[111] On 12 April, this group entered the Doon Valley. It crossed the site of the future Cantonment of Dehradun, and then climbed out of the valley and went slightly to the east of what would, in another twenty years, become the hill station of Mussoorie. From the Landour Ridge, Hearsey and the others got their first good look at the giants of the Garhwal Himalayas.

A 1910 postcard showing snow covered mountain ranges as visible from Mussoorie.

(Dehradun: Survey of India, 1950), 73.

[109]Pearse H., *The Hearseys: Five Generations of an Anglo-Indian Family* (London: William Blackwood and Sons, 1905), 56.

[110]Although of British origin, he was given the name of Hyder. His second name is originally believed to have been Jung, which he later changed to Young. Ibid, 38.

[111]Phillimore R.H., *Historical Records of Survey of India: Vol II, 1800 to 1815* (Dehradun: Survey of India, 1950), 74.

Just to complete the tale of this quest to Gangotri, this party reached the village of Raithal (79 kilometres from Gangotri), beyond which the steep and narrow hill paths halted their progress. However, Webb dispatched one of his workers (a munshi) to complete the quest to Gangotri.[112] It was the munshi's account that dispelled the myth that Ganges originated from Mansarovar.

Now a small history regarding Hearsey: he was an exceptional soldier and commander who, by 1811, owned the entire territory of Dehradun! Hearsey persuaded the exiled King of Garhwal, Sudarshan Shah, to sell him the territory of Dehradun and Chandi for a paltry sum of ₹3,005. Although he managed to sell Chandi to British for a sum of ₹1,200, the British refused to accept Hearsey's claims on Dehradun.

Cloud's End

Fairy tales happen for real, and poems come to life! Just ask the old-timers of Mussoorie and they may rhapsodically narrate the tale of a British soldier and a Garhwali belle.

'Have you read the poem "The Solitary Reaper" by William Wordsworth?' asked Mr M, an old-timer,[113] as I sat with pen and notepad in hand, waiting eagerly for some golden words and ancient knowledge about our town.

'Read it in standard four or five, found the English very difficult, vaguely remember getting scolded by my teacher.' I mumbled.

'What is the theme of the poem?' Mr M pressed.

'Well, it's about a girl who is singing in a corn field and the poet happens to hear her song. Gets pretty impressed and writes

---

[112]Ibid, 75.

[113]Mr M was a treasure trove of local stories, anecdotes and titbits. His help in shaping my book is gratefully acknowledged. But as per his directions, I am not disclosing his name.

a damn poem,' I blurted (with all due respect to the learned Wordsworth). 'But I am sure it's fiction,' I added defensively.

'My boy, let me narrate a real story to you. Very similar to "The Solitary Reaper" and much closer to home,' he said with a twinkle in his eyes.

Here's the story Mr M told me (I have added some details based on my subsequent research).

Major Swetenham, a British officer in command of the Landour Cantonment[114], and his friends were out for a shikar (hunt) in the forests to the west of Mussoorie. As the tired party sat down under the shade of some oak trees, a woman's voice echoed through the forest. The song was in the local tongue; something the goras didn't understand, but the voice was melodious.

Swetenham took off in the direction of the voice. A few moments later, he was able to spot a young village girl singing a lullaby. Immersed in her song, at first the girl didn't notice the stranger listening to her. When he emerged from the thicket and stood right in front of her, the startled belle ran away. But Cupid had struck! Smitten by the beauty of this Garhwali belle, Swetenham ran in pursuit.

The girl happened to be a resident of Kandi village and

A mid-nineteenth century portrait of Major Edmund Swetenham (1795–1863) who married a local Garhwali girl called Gulabo (nee Rose) and had built Cloud's End. He had five sons—Charles, Edmund, George, Robert Alexander and Henry Harvey, and three daughters—Rose, Elizabeth Frances and Isabella. (Picture courtesy: Richard Swetenham)

---

[114]Earlier referred to as the 'Invalids Establishment of Landour'.

turned out to be the only daughter of a Garhwali landlord. It apparently took some persuasion by Swetenham to convince the landlord to give him his daughter's hand in marriage.

Gulabo, the village belle, soon became Mrs Rose Swetenham, the wife of a senior British army officer. The generous landlord gave his entire estate—extending hundreds of acres, up to the hills of Bhadraj—as dowry, and the British army officer became a landlord! A happy ending indeed.

But the tale is not finished yet. Swetenham named the estate Cloud's End—after the name of a peak in his native village. A house was built at Cloud's End in 1838.

Traveller Fanny Parks—who happened to be an acquaintance of the Major and was on a visit to Mussoorie—was entrusted with

The Swetenham family at Cloud's End in 1912. Standing: Adelaide Eliza McCutchan (1846–1917) and her husband Colonel Robert Alexander Swetenham (1845–1913). Sitting (L to R): 1) their daughter Hazel Adelaide Swetenham (1889–1918); 2) Emily Kathleen Kelly née Raynor (1882–1967); 3) their daughter Edith Rose Swetenham (1882–1963). (Photo courtesy: Digvijay Aggarwal)

the responsibility of supervising the construction work. Parks writes in her journal about her periodic visits to Cloud's End, about the progress of construction and about organizing parties at the estate.

My friend and current owner of Cloud's End Estate Mr Digvijay Aggarwal, is quick to point out that he had found an 'antique' bottle opener at the tent site once described by Fanny Parks. 'I have kept that opener in my museum at the estate. Perhaps it was used by Fanny to open beer and wine bottles.' Mr Aggarwal quips.

Returning to the Swetenham couple, they had settled at Cloud's End and had five sons. All sons served as colonels in the British army. One of them, Colonel R.A. Swetenham, was a signatory to the charter of the Dehradun Club when it was converted into a limited company in 1901. One granddaughter inherited her grandma's voice and became one of Mussoorie's most popular 'nightingales'.[115]

In 1965, the estate was sold to Mr Durga Ram Agarwal for ₹37,000. His son, Digvijay Aggarwal, now runs a resort at the sprawling estate that spans 400 acres. 'The old

A studio photo of Clement Alfred Swetenham at Mussoorie in 1909, aged about 3. His mother has written 'my jhampani' on the cover. Also noticeable is a small jhampan with a teddy bear kept on the ground. (Photographer: J.H. Dagg; Photo courtesy: Richard Swetenham)

---

[115]Hari Har Lal P., *The Doon Valley Down the Ages* (New Delhi: Interprint, 1993), 176.

building is still intact, the drawing room windows are still there in original,' he assures me. He also maintains a museum.

Located to the east of Bhadraj, around seven kilometres from Gandhi Chowk, the drive to Cloud's End is through serene and picturesque forests. Cloud's End offers a magnificent view of the Himalayan snow peaks and the nearby mountain ranges.

Sir George Everest's Home in the Himalayas

The Park Estate—located towards the southwest of Cloud's End— was once the home of Mussoorie's most distinguished resident. The man after whom the world's tallest peak is named.

Yes! The Park was the home of Colonel Sir George Everest, Surveyor General of India and Superintendent of Great Trigonometric Survey, the man under whose leadership the Great Meridional Arc—from Cape Comorin to the Himalayas—was measured, based on which distances and heights in the Indian subcontinent were calculated.

Everest's moment of fame arrived long after he had hung up his boots when the world's tallest peak (formerly known as 'Peak XV') was named after him.

However, Everest did not measure the height of Mount Everest; this pioneering feat was achieved by Radhanath Sikdar, a brilliant mathematician working as 'Chief Computer' with the Survey of India. In those days, manual calculating machines were used to aid humans, and the person operating such machines was referred to as the 'computer'. So, our human computer, Radhanath Sikdar, had a 'eureka!' moment in 1852 when he discovered that Peak XV was actually the highest peak in the world.

In 1856, the then Surveyor General of India and protégé of Everest, Andrew Waugh, recommended naming this peak after Sir George Everest and, in 1865, the peak was so proclaimed by the Royal Geographical Society.

During my brief engagement with NIAR,[116] Mussoorie, I remember taking a group of Civil Service Officers from Bangladesh to the Everest house and having an interesting discussion with them.

'The height of Everest was calculated by a Bengali not by Everest. But our Bangla brother never got any credit!' exclaimed one of the officers while the others grunted in agreement.

But let me overcome my emotions and come back to our discussion about Sir George Everest. Everest, who had been appointed the Surveyor General of India as well as the Superintendent of the Great Trigonometric Survey, arrived at The Park on 10 May 1832 and lived here until 1843.

A 2015 picture of the ruins of the house of Sir George Everest. The original house was much larger but a major part of the original house was demolished by subsequent owners in the late 1970s–1980s. Now the entire building has been demolished and replaced by a new building by the Tourism Department of Uttarakhand.

---

[116]National Institute of Administrative Research (NIAR), now renamed as Centre for Good Governance (CEGG), is engaged in research as well as training programmes for civil servants. I was engaged by NIAR to give lectures on the history of Mussoorie.

Sir Everest had purchased this estate from a fellow officer in the Bengal Artillery called Colonel Whish.[117] Whish had bought The Park Estate in 1829, and the house, constructed on the estate in 1829–1830, is regarded as one of the earliest houses in the town. Everest had purchased The Park, which was a large estate spread over 920 acres, for a hefty sum of money.

His house at The Park was huge; consisting of a large hall, a semicircular drawing room and eleven other rooms, including several bedrooms, two kitchens and two bathrooms. This sprawling mansion offered a breathtaking view of the Himalayas towards the northeast, and that of the Doon Valley towards the south. A large oval pond towards the southwest of the building provided water for irrigating a large farm where potatoes were cultivated. Mr Arvind Shah, whose family had owned the house in the later years, tells me that there was also a cricket ground on the estate and matches were frequently held there.

During my innumerable visits to The Park, I have often imagined Everest sitting in his study, gazing down at the picturesque Doon Valley, sipping vintage wine. What joy it must have been to live in such vistas—taking early morning strolls in the forests, or gazing at the sunsets in the evening, scrambling up the nearby Hathipaon Hill (7029 metres [23,061 feet] above sea level) for a change in scenery, or an occasional horse ride to the Mall!

But the hardworking Everest had little time for such pleasures. He once wrote about being tied down to the desk, 'like a slave to the oar, from mornings sometimes till midnight'.

The biggest challenge at The Park was scarcity of water, and Everest had engaged eight mules to fetch water daily from the Whish's Well (see Wishing Well later in this chapter), located a kilometre away. A roof water harvesting system was designed

---

[117]Colonel William Sampson Whish (1787–1853) retired as Lieutenant General in the Bengal Artillery.

and rainwater was collected in an underground reservoir—105 feet long, 5 feet wide and 6 feet deep—the excess being allowed to flow into the pond.

Everest spent part of his summers and the rainy season at The Park, while moving down to the office of Survey at Dehradun after the rains, dividing his time at Dehradun between office work and field visits to various locations for the Great Trigonometrical Survey. Everest allowed his staff to build a temporary settlement at The Park. In 1839, the government allowed Everest to construct a temporary observatory and workshop.

After spending over ten years at Mussoorie, Everest left in September 1843 and got all temporary buildings dismantled and sold. The great surveyor finally sailed for England from Calcutta on 16 December 1843.

Everest had appointed Captain Murray, one of his neighbours, as his attorney to sell The Park. However, The Park continued to be in Everest's ownership until it was sold to a Colonel Robert Thatcher in 1861. Around 1870, Thatcher sold The Park to Colonel James

A late nineteenth century postcard showing a scene on The Park Estate; the caption says 'At the Park Gate.' (Photo courtesy: Hotel Savoy, Mussoorie)

Skinner, who was keen to build his residence here. But Skinner had to sell it soon as his family did not like the remote location of The Park. The local brewer, John Mackinnon, purchased The Park from Skinner, and his descendants sold it to a local resident, Inder Lal Shah, in 1943 along with 920 acres of adjoining estate.

Mr Shah's family resided in this house until 1966, and his son Arvind Shah, who grew up at The Park, has fond memories of this house.

'The underground reservoir was functional when we moved into the house. Leopard and other wildlife sightings were common. It was fun to spend the childhood here,' Mr Arvind recalls.

Mr Arvind also recalls that in July 1961, lightning struck the house twice—damaging a large portion of the building on the north side.

The Shahs sold The Park to Mr Puran Singh of Dehradun and later, in the mid-1990s, this building was purchased by the tourism department.

The tourism department has allocated ₹24 crore to renovate the house of Sir George Everest—reconstructing the demolished building, making a museum, amphitheatre, star-gazing site and what not. We do hope that the old rustic charm of the house will be preserved.

Everest's tiffs with Young

Everest was indomitable—like the tallest peak named after him. He never cowed from a fight if his personal honour was at stake, or even if it was in defence of a subordinate officer. During his eleven-year stint in the Doon Valley, Everest was said to have been on 'most friendly'[118] terms with Captain Young,[119] but he did have

---

[118]Phillimore, R.H., *Historical Records of Survey of India: Vol. IV, 1830 to 1843* (Dehradun: Survey of India, 1958), 435.

[119]Who, by this time, had been elevated to Superintendent of Doon.

his share of disputes with Young over official matters. Young, who had risen to the post of Lieutenant Colonel and was the 'political agent' of Dehradun from 1833 to 1842, was four years senior to Everest—in age as well as in commission into the army.[120]

Compasswala Saheb[121]

In December 1834, Everest received an application for a pension from an Indian worker. This application had been forwarded to him by Young—the political agent—with his covering letter.

The Indian worker had used the native term, 'Compasswala Saheb'—a term generally used to refer to surveyors—while addressing Everest, and this infuriated the Surveyor General. He immediately wrote to Young. 'I am not a Compasswala but Surveyor General and Superintendent of the Great Trigonometrical Survey of India.' Adding that he never gave nicknames to anyone and always respected others and that he had a right, 'to look for equal courtesy in return.'

The ever-diplomatic Young replied with tact that although he had not noticed anything disrespectful in the letter— 'Compasswala' was common parlance to refer to surveyors—he had issued directions in his office to prevent such occurrence in the future. 'I have given directions that no public document shall pass my office in which you are designated by any other title than Surveyor General Saheb Bahadur,' Young said in his reply.

Everest retorted that he was addressed by the title of 'Surveyor General Kishwar Hind' and he would be obliged if this title was used for addressing him.

---

[120]Phillimore R.H., *Historical Records of Survey of India: Vol. IV, 1830 to 1843* (Dehradun: Survey of India, 1958), 167.
[121]Ibid.

The Wayward Mule

This hilarious incident took place at the Survey of India office at Dehradun, which shared a boundary with the office and residence of Henry Kirke, station officer of Sirmoor Battalion.

Everest's aide, Charles Morrison, was posted at the Survey office. One fine day, Morrison's mule wandered into Kirke's premises. It was promptly captured by Kirke's men and tied up in the Battalion office.

Morrison wrote a letter to Kirke, requesting for the mule's release while offering to pay for any damages caused. Kirke replied by demanding a fine of two annas,[122] which was promptly paid by Morrison to secure the 'release' of the mule.

Shortly afterwards, a herd of cattle belonging to Kirke ventured into the Survey premises and merrily nibbled away at the grass-thatched huts of the Survey officials. Morrison's men managed to catch four of the errant cattle, which were duly tied up in the Survey office. Morrison expected that Kirke would pay a fine similar to what Morrison had paid for his mule.

Morrison was taken aback when Kirke sent a Hawaldar instead, with four sepoys 'wielding bayonets', who entered the Survey premises and forcibly released the cattle.

Morrison then wrote a lengthy letter to Everest, narrating the entire incident and even sharing the copies of the correspondence between him and Kirke. Morrison further added fuel to the fire by mentioning that Kirke had replaced the Hawaldar at the Survey's treasury and that the new Hawaldar was refusing to obey orders.

This brought 'fire to Everest's pen' and he immediately reported the matter to the commander-in-chief of the Bengal army, with a copy to Young forcing an apology from both Young and Kirke.

---

[122]Equal to 12.50 paise

Country liquor

Everest and Young had yet another spat, this time over the brewing of country liquor by the khalasis[123] employed in the Survey department.

Young, who was also the controller of excise, wrote to Everest that without a government license it was unlawful to brew country liquor. He mentioned that the government had given license to two Indians to brew and sell local liquor, and requested Everest to facilitate the opening of a liquor shop in Survey campus so that illicit brewing could stop.

Everest retorted by mentioning that in his regiment the soldiers were barred from accessing liquor shops.

But Young persisted, and threatened to report the matter to the Commissioner.

Never one to back down, Everest asked Young to show the rule by which Everest was bound to open a liquor shop in the Survey premises. He never got a reply from Young.

Wishing Well

A well, located on the boundary of The Park, is known as the 'Wishing Well'. Hordes of tourists—guided by our town's knowledgeable informers—drop a penny into the well and make a wish. On my first visit to this well, even I was beguiled into dropping a coin and making a wish!

A newspaper once made an outrageous claim that Abhishek Bachchan had once dropped a coin into the well and wished for his marriage with Aishwarya.

Another claim doing the rounds these days is that a person must stand with their back to the well, and then throw the coin over the shoulder—the wish will be fulfilled if the coin drops

---

[123]The support staff.

A recent picture of the Wishing Well. This well was the source of drinking water for the household of Sir George Everest and is still in use by nearby villagers.

into the water without hitting the inner walls of the well. Quite ingenious! Perhaps this is how urban legends are born.

Definitely, this myth has not been created by the villagers from nearby settlements who get their daily supply of water from this well. Although a young man once told me that he doesn't mind making a little extra income by retrieving the coins dropped into the well.

Actually, this well was constructed by Colonel Whish of The Park Estate in 1829–1830 to meet household drinking water requirements. Later, it was used by Sir George Everest who had kept eight mules to fetch drinking water. For over a century now, the well has been the primary source of water for the nearby village communities.

Constructed by Colonel Whish, this well was originally known as 'Whish's Well'. I have no clue how and when it was rechristened the 'Wishing Well' with the added fable of 'drop a penny and make a wish'.

Not wanting to deprive local lads of their pocket money—I would still urge all readers to make a visit to 'Whish's Well'. Do drop a penny and make a wish. Nothing wrong in making an earnest wish—remember Paulo Coelho, 'And, when you want something, all the universe conspires in helping you to achieve it.'

Benog

The peak of Benog[124] (2.250 m [7,433[125] feet]) was the terminal station for the triangulation survey being conducted under Sir George Everest—it formed the reference point for the calculation of height of other peaks of the Garhwal range.

But Benog is even more famous as the last known residence of the Himalayan bush quail (*Ophrysia superciliosa*)—a rare bird that has not been spotted for the past 145 years.

A young boy, Kenneth Mackinnon, apparently from the famous Mackinnon family of brewers, made the first recorded sighting of this bird near Benog in November 1865. On a hunting trip with a pack of dogs, Kenneth's dogs flushed out a flock of eight to ten birds from their hideout amongst tall grass on the mountain slope.

Kenneth was able to shoot two birds, one of which he gave to a Colonel L'Estrange. He apparently devoured one of the birds, but seemingly without much relish. In a letter to Hume, Kenneth explains that the birds were small in size and only capable of short flights and had tasted poor. 'Their flight was slow and heavy, and I should never have supposed them capable of migrating far. I attached neither importance nor value to them, or I might have shot more, but they were very small birds, and involved an immense deal of bother in shooting (and proved, I may add,

---

[124]During the nineteenth century, it was referred to as 'Ben Oge'.
[125]Height calculated in nineteenth century was 7,524.20 feet.

poor eating),' Kenneth wrote.[126]

He reported spotting these birds 'occasionally' and hearing the shrill whistling sound made by them, but he did not bother hunting them anymore, '[...] having ascertained what they were like, I troubled myself no further about them,' he wrote to Hume.

During 1867 and 1868, Captain Hutton[127] spotted the Himalayan quail near Jharipani, and apparently shot at least four birds. Last sighting in Mussoorie was by Hutton in June 1868, and the only other sighting was in Nainital in 1876.

Only nine specimens of this elusive bird exist today in various museums around the world. Oh, dear Kenneth, you shouldn't have eaten one of the birds.

The mountain quail is the holy grail for birders in India, and several unsuccessful attempts have been made to search for this species—including one by noted ornithologist Dr Salim Ali in 1977.

The International Union for Conservation of Nature (IUCN) has listed the mountain quail in the 'critically endangered, possibly extinct' category.

Meanwhile, Benog Mountain Quail Bird Sanctuary was established in 1993—a good step, I must say, to prevent wanton hunting in the area. Covering an area of 339 hectares, Benog still remains a heaven for birdwatchers, and the last bird survey reported sighting of ninety birds, including white-capped redstart, red-billed blue magpie, Himalayan shrike-babbler, goldcrest and the penegrine falcon. Hopefully, the Himalayan quail might turn up someday, who knows!

---

[126]Hume A.O. & Marshall C.H.T., *The Game Birds of India, Burmah and Ceylon: Vol. II.* (Calcutta: Central Press Co. Ltd, 1879), 106.

[127]Captain Hutton also introduced sericulture to Mussoorie in 1858, after which Messrs Lister & Company took up commercial production of silk in a village in Dehradun, which is today known as Resham Majri. Hutton was also reported to have collected a specimen of a rare bat at Jharipani—the Peter's tube-nosed bat (*Harpiola grisea*) named after German biologist W. Peters.

Located in close proximity to Cloud's End and Everest house, Benog is ideal for a day-trip and, apart from the birds, it offers scenic vistas and some splendid snow-peak views. Early birds can get some of the most amazing views of sunrise.

Nachne-wali Mem[128]

Mr Digvijay Aggarwal told me that after his father bought the Cloud's End Estate in 1965, their family hardly ever visited the place. A chowkidar used to take care of the estate with some cousins of Aggarwal visiting now and then.

In 1981, the chowkidar ran away, apparently with some valuables stolen from the house. On hearing this, Mr Aggarwal, who was in his twenties, had to rush to the estate.

'I must have reached the estate around 3 p.m. in the afternoon. I distinctly remember the date—it was 10 January 1981,' he narrates. Shortly after, some villagers from nearby Bhandiyala and Dudhli villages, who were passing by, noticed him at the estate.

'Who are you? What are you doing here?' one of them asked.

'I am the owner of this estate,' he replied.

'But we thought the owner was the chowkidar. He had told us that the British owner had willed the property to him,' retorted the villager.

After explaining the facts to the concerned villagers and making their acquaintance, Mr Aggarwal said he would stay at the house for a few days.

'Are you alone?' they asked in unison.

'Yes, but how does it matter?' Mr Aggarwal replied.

'Do not stay here alone, saheb, it is not safe. A mem comes and dances here in the middle of the night,' the villagers cautioned.

Undeterred, Mr Aggarwal told them that it was his house and he would spend the night in it.

Not convinced, one of the villagers asked, 'Do you have a gun?'

---

[128]'Mem' is a colloquial term used in India to refer to foreign women.

'I do not have a gun and if I did, it would be of little use against a ghost,' Mr Aggarwal quipped.

He told me that he slept soundly after having a packed dinner that he had brought from home at Dehradun. Around 2 a.m., a rustling sound woke him.

'I jumped to my feet but the sound seemed to have stopped,' he said. 'As I lay down on my bed, I heard the sound again. It seemed like someone was gently tapping on the door or window. There was no electricity in the house, you see. We got electricity years later. Back then, we used candles, torches and gas lamps,' he narrates.

Mr Aggarwal fumbled for a torch and, opening the door of his bedroom, followed the sound, which seemed to be coming from the living room.

'There was no trace of the "*nachne wali mem*" in the living room. I was disappointed.' he told me with a wide smile on his face.

But he could still hear the sound; it seemed to be coming from the window.

'I tried to peek through the window, but it was too dark to make out anything.'

Finally, in the morning, he set out to explore and found that a creeper rose had rambled up the wall just outside the living room window and that its leaves were rustling with the blowing wind.

'I have been living in this house for forty years now, still waiting for a rendezvous with the "*nachne wali mem*",' he says with a laugh.

5

CAMEL ATOP THE HILL

'How did the Brits manage to get a camel up these hills?' asked my cousin from the United Kingdom on his maiden visit to Mussoorie as I took him for a stroll on Camel's Back Road one evening.

'Who said anything about a camel here?' I questioned.

'Well, it was named Camel's Back Road. Must have been a camel around at some point.' he argued.

'Yes, indeed there was a camel,' I laughed. 'But not a real one, just a rock shaped like a camel,' I added.

This picturesque road runs parallel to the Mall and is believed to be named after a camel-shaped natural rock formation that rests on a hill that lies alongside the road.

But wait, there's another camel around! This winding road is actually shaped like the two humps of a camel—try Google Maps and see.

Taking a Walk

Morning or evening strolls on Camel's Back—a level walk of three kilometres, offering a magnificent view of the Himalayan ranges—are most enjoyable, especially with pleasant company.

Clear blue skies, interspersed with white clouds, and the chirping of birds atop the banj[129] trees—which are still, as there is no breeze to ruffle them—welcome the early risers during April and May.

In the monsoons, clouds rise from the valley below, and a white blanket of mist engulfs the road, planting gentle kisses on

---

[129]*Quercus leucotrichophora*

the face of strollers.

During September and October, one can see wild dahlias in full bloom on the slopes of Camel Hill. Crimson, pink, purple, yellow, blue, white—just take your pick.

An early twentieth century scene of a snow-covered Camel's Back Road. The man standing in the centre has a shovel in hand and is making a pathway. (Photographer: Julian Rust)

A Horse Ride?

The British favoured Camel's Back Road for equestrian pursuits— but with horses cantering and galloping on the narrow winding road, accidents were not uncommon.

A young lady, cantering merrily on horseback, had a lucky escape near Scandal Point. As she approached a small bridge covering a deep gorge, she realized that the overnight rains had washed away the bridge. Too late to pull up! She spurred her horse and jumped across the chasm.[130]

---

[130]Northam J., *Guide to Masuri, Landaur, Dehradun and The Hills North of Dehra* (Calcutta: Thacker, Spink and Co., 1884), 35.

John Lang[131] also mentions the narrow escape of a British couple who were out horse riding on this road.

'A few years ago, a lady and a gentleman were riding round a place called Camel's Back; the road gave way, and they fell several hundred feet down the precipice. The horses were killed, but the riders miraculously escaped with only a few severe bruises,' Lang writes.

The tradition of horse riding on Camel's Back Road continued over the years, even as British riders were replaced by scores of Indian tourists.

Poor pedestrians had to wade across mounds of 'horse apples' while evading the bolting horses with their animated riders. It was difficult to judge who was in control—the horse or the rider!

Behind the horse came the owner—scooting along—trying to run faster than the animal to grab the reins. Thankfully, horse riding was banned about a decade ago.

The Scandal Point

Entering Camel's Back Road while coming from Gandhi Chowk, a walk of about 500 metres, brings one to a rustic looking green canopy, mounted on antique cast-iron pillars. Few benches underneath the canopy are almost perpetually occupied by tourists or locals who take delight in watching the scenic Aglar Valley below.

It offers some amazing views of the Nag Tibba towards the north with a backdrop of snow-clad Bandarpunch (6,316 m [20,722 feet]) and Swargarohini (6,252 m [20,512 feet]) ranges. Orange, crimson and mauve hues in the sky at the time of sunset are a splendid sight too.

This place is now called The Bahuguna Park. But it is actually the famous 'Scandal Point' of yesteryears. It was a meeting place

---

[131]Lang J., *The Mahommedan Mother* in Dickens C. (ed.), *Household Words: Vol. VII, Magazine No. 168*, 11 June 1853, 339.

Scandal Point in the early 1960s.

for young lovers and hence the name. It has been given an innocuous name now as its original name was perhaps too 'scandalous' to suit the Indian gentry. About 500 metres from Scandal Point is the Christian Cemetery, where many notable citizens of yore are resting in peace (see chapter 7).

Camel Atop the Hill

About 200 metres beyond the cemetery, we finally arrive at the 'Camel point'—a small shack with a few telescopes lined along the road mark this spot. One can see the rock shaped camel on the hill bordering the road.

The hill on which the camel rock lies is referred to as Camel's Hill or Gun Hill. '[...] almost perfect natural statue in rock of a camel crouched down on his knees and haunches, laden to the full. This small piece of rock, so fashioned in nature's own mound, gave, they say, the hill on which it rests the name it bears,'[132] observes John Northam, in one of the earliest guide books on Mussoorie.

Due to the abundance of 'game', forests below Camel's Back Road continued to be much favoured hunting grounds for British and Indian shikaris (hunters) till the early 1980s—with hunting parties bragging at length about their exploits of shooting pheasants, or even managing to hunt a deer or the rare Himalayan goral.[133]

---

[132]Northam J., *Guide to Masuri, Landaur, Dehradun and The Hills North of Dehra* (Calcutta: Thacker, Spink and Co., 1884), 39.

[133]The Himalayan goral (*Naemorhedus goral*) also called a small goat antelope,

Among the amateurs, a sudden visit by a curious leopard or a bear led to mayhem. There is one such anecdote from the 1950s about two greenhorns, a Mr J and a Mr B (refraining from taking names as they are no more today, but I knew them very well); one of them picked up his father's gun, and off they went—merrily descending into the forests below the cemetery. Elated after bagging a few wild fowls on their maiden hunt, the two youngsters had barely turned back when they heard a deep growl.

'Get up the tree; get up the tree!' both shouted in unison. Luckily, a large oak tree was at hand, and the alacrity with which both hunters scrambled up the tree would have put a monkey to shame. Barely had they managed to climb a large bough that a big leopard emerged from the underbrush.

'As the leopard gazed upward at us, I pointed the gun at him. I swear to God, I would have blown its brains out but for the stupidity of my friend who fidgeted and struck his elbow on my hand, causing me to drop the gun,' narrated one the hunters, accompanied by strong protests from his companion.

'He was trembling and his gun dropped from his hand. I had asked him to hand the gun to me but he was too scared,' the companion maintained over the next several years.

Thankfully, the leopard did not climb up the tree as he was more interested in their bag full of wild fowls that lay on the ground. After the leopard sauntered off with his lunch, the two shikaris waited for several hours before they could gather the courage to climb down the tree.

I am told that the two friends were mocked for a long time for their eventful hunting expedition, and whenever this discussion came up, the two buddies invariably broke into an argument

is found in the Himalayas at heights above 2,000 metres (6,561 feet). It is of short stature, has a yellowish-grey and black coat and small conical horns. It has now been listed as 'Near Threatened' species on the IUCN Red List.

about how the gun was dropped.

Leopards still frequent Camel's Back Road and, just a few years ago, a CCTV camera at Nirankari Bhawan captured a large leopard strolling on the road at night. Many residents also claim to have seen the large cat—many a times with cubs—near the cemetery or on the slopes above the Aglar Valley. But God bless the forest officials who have managed to keep the hunters at bay.

Close to this place was once the Mussoorie Volunteer Rifle Corps with a 500-yard firing point.[134] Raised in 1871, this corps had a strength of 201. It comprised of four companies—one of them being the 'St. George's College Cadet Company'.

Further ahead is a narrow lane climbing steeply upwards to meet Mall Road near the post office and telephone exchange. This is the Lavender Lane, or more commonly known as 'Taar Gali'. The name, Taar Gali, is understandable because this lane borders the telegraph office. But why Lavender Lane? Especially since I have never come across any lavender trees in the vicinity.

I have often heard of the phrase 'paying through the teeth', but its literal meaning dawned upon me when I came to know about a gentleman who had to give his dentist a large chunk of prime land as a fee for receiving a set of dentures.

Dr Miller, the beneficiary, promptly built a huge skating rink on this land in 1890—naming it 'The Rink'.[135] Located at the entrance to Camel's Back Road from Kulri Bazaar, the rink was the first building in the town to be lighted by acetylene lamps. Once regarded as the largest skating rink in north India, this remained a popular hangout for youngsters till the 1990s.

---

[134]Northam J., *Guide to Masuri, Landaur, Dehradun and The Hills North of Dehra* (Calcutta: Thacker, Spink and Co., 1884), 39 and 54.

[135]Hari Har Lal P., *The Doon Valley Down the Ages* (New Delhi: Interprint, 1993), 181.

A 1904 postcard showing The Rink building on Camel's Back Road. (Photographer: C. Nickels)

Once quaint, serene and picturesque, Camel's Back Road of yesteryears now becomes a car park during the busy summers—although the stretch between the cemetery and Scandal Point still offers some peace and wonderful views.

Don't venture out after nightfall!

'Doors were securely bolted after sunset. People were wary of visitors after dark, easily started by sudden noises and avoided venturing out,' informs Mr Gopal Bhardwaj, a noted historian and a resident of Camel's Back Road.

Fears arose due to lack of habitation in this area, the presence of a cemetery and even the threat of wild animals, particularly leopards.

Several stories were doing the rounds that reinforced the fears of the residents. Strange sightings and occurrences, strange noises and other unexplained events were also frequently reported.

Each such report made the 'believers' pray even longer and issue stricter dictums to children. Although many self-proclaimed 'rational' ones blatantly dismissed such reports.

Let me share few of the most scary and popular stories.

Mr B's encounter

Mr Bhardwaj narrates an unusual encounter, told to him by a Mr Baretto, who resided in a cottage near the present-day Nirankari Bhawan (adjoining the cemetery).

Mr Baretto was an Anglo-Indian, a thorough gentleman and a devout Christian. Every day, he dutifully returned home—a twenty-minute walk from his workplace on the Mall—by sunset.

One evening, in the 1940s, Mr B was caught up in work and was late in leaving his establishment. As he hurried back home, he took the Lavender Lane from the Mall.

'Mr Baretto later said that as soon as he started on the lane, he felt a surge of unexplained fear. It was as if something was amiss!' Mr Bhardwaj says.

As he reached the junction of Lavender Lane and Camel's Back Road, a voice in his mind told him to turn back. He increased his pace and hurried ahead. He was barely twenty metres from the cemetery when he noticed a silhouette just outside the gate. Abruptly stopping in his tracks, Mr B stared fearfully and was able to make out an unusually tall Englishman standing at the gate.

'The man was at least ten feet tall, attired in a suit and a bowler hat, and was staring menacingly at Mr Baretto,' says Mr Bhardwaj.

Trembling with fear, Mr B, who always kept a Bible upon his person, had the presence of mind to dig it out from his pocket and start reading randomly from the holy book. Mr Bhardwaj says that Mr B swore by the holy spirit that he saw 'the apparition dissolve into thin air'.

Miss L and the Englishmen

In the 1960s, a middle-aged teacher, Miss Lal, lived alone in a house. In those days, Camel's Back Road was a terribly secluded place to live. And as if this wasn't enough to instil a feeling of eeriness, especially during dark, whispery nights, her house overlooked the cemetery, further deepening her hollow feeling of loneliness, making her wary about her surroundings.

Although a pucca socialite, the spinster preferred to finish her social sojourns and return to her house before sunset. One evening, Miss Lal was unusually late, and as dusk was setting in, she was ambling towards her house. As she was walking past the gate of the cemetery, she came upon a tall Englishman. Her eyes flitted over his attire—an immaculately well-ironed dark suit, a perfectly knotted red tie and a black hat, tilting a wee bit to the left. He struck up a conversation with her, and she delightfully obliged.

He wished her in a gentlemanly manner, and then asked for directions to the Mall Road. He went on to explain that it'd been years since he'd last visited Mussoorie. And as the town had undergone a considerable transformation, he had lost his bearings.

During the short conversation, Miss L was impressed by the courteous Englishman; after all, it was rare to find such a strikingly handsome bloke strolling aimlessly on her side of town.

It was all good, except for one little detail—something about his bloodshot eyes pinched her as strange—which she mentioned to her friends later when she narrated the entire account. Finding that a bit odd for such a well-groomed individual, she let it slide, attributing it to lack of sleep.

Miss L went on with her routine life. The handsome man she had met escaped her thoughts. But this is when things began to change dramatically—and not in a good way.

She became the focus of some sinister occurrences, things she'd never heard or witnessed in the town ever before. And they were happening in her house! The light of her bedroom would turn on automatically in the middle of the night; she would hear strange whistling sounds from outside the door; and she swore that one evening she saw a shadow lurking outside her window. Whose shadow was it? Was it the tall English bloke she had met? Or was it the silhouette of anyone she knew? What about the eyes... were they bloodshot too? These questions remained unanswered as a terrified lady could not stay for long at that house, and she promptly packed her bags and left—never to return again.

This story still fascinates many locals. But they just wildly speculate about the link between the Englishmen near the cemetery—who had found the surroundings to have changed—and the strange occurrences. And, if it's any consolation, these weren't the first—and surely won't be the last—mysteries of Mussoorie whose answer ended up buried in the dense forests of the town or floated away with a blanket of fog.

But let me assure my readers that I have moved around Camel's Back at late hours, even after midnight, and at times alone, and I am yet to have an encounter with any Englishman.

Gun Hill

Since 1865, after a gun (cannon) was mounted on the top of Camel's Back hill, this hillock is more popularly referred as the 'Gun Hill'. The cannon was supplied by the Cossipore Ordinance Factory (Calcutta). Charged with moist grass, cotton waste and gun powder, the barrel was fired towards the Doon Valley daily at noon, 'ostensibly' to indicate the time—but perhaps more of a brazen announcement of the pomp and grandeur of a colonial empire.

The person who operated this gun appears to have been a mighty disgruntled bloke. Whether he was unhappy due to his measly pay of 12 pence a day, or due to general inactivity (his only job being firing the cannon once a day) or, graver still, he might be having trouble with the missus—your guess is as good as mine. But the misadventures of the gun operator do indicate that something was amiss.

The canon at Gun Hill being fired sometime in the early nineteenth century. The person crouching behind the gun, covering his ears, seems to be the 'misadventuring' gun operator. (Picture courtesy: Hotel Savoy, Mussoorie)

One fine day, he 'forgot' to remove the ramrod[136] from the barrel, and when the gun boomed at noon, 'it sent the ramrod clean through the roof of Stella cottage!'[137]

On another day, an 'accidental' overcharge of powder in the cannon sent the cannon ball soaring towards Rajpur. Absolute pandemonium followed! The cotton ball landed right in the lap of a lady being carried in a dandi to Rajpur.[138] Thankfully, the poor lady did not die of fright.

---

[136]A ramrod is a wooden or metal stick used to push the projectile inside the barrel of a canon or a gun.

[137]The Rambler, *A Mussoorie Miscellany* (Mussoorie: Mafasilite Press, 1936), 48.

[138]Ibid.

After World War I, the British launched an economic drive that led to the silencing of the gun in 1919. The cannon continued to stand proudly as a mute sentinel on Gun Hill until 1940,[139] when its barrel was removed and sent to the melting pot. God knows what became of the carriage wheels that continued to stand forlornly on the hill.

So now we have a 'Gun Hill' sans a gun! But Gun Hill still continues to maintain its importance as the main water reservoir of the town. A huge water reservoir, built by hollowing out the hilltop, has a capacity of over 17 million litres and supplies water to most of the town. It is replenished by pumping water from nearby springs.

The head office of the Great Trigonometrical Survey was located at Mussoorie. Initially, it was at Montrose on Camel's Back Road, and was later shifted to Evelyn Hall, near the top of Gun Hill. At some point, Sir George Everest is believed to have worked from this office, which had an observatory with a big 36-inch theodolite. It was later shifted to Dehradun. Evelyn Hall was later transformed into a nursing home.

Around 1970, the Municipal Board got a ropeway constructed from the Mall Road to the top of Gun Hill—transforming the reservoir into a popular tourist attraction. From the top, tourists can feast their eyes on some of the most spectacular views of snow-clad peaks to the north, and of Mussoorie and the Doon Valley. Close to a hundred shacks on the top of Gun Hill offer refreshments, games and joy rides for children.

There are also photography shops at Gun Hill; with their 'fancy dresses' they attract those with a flair for dressing. The victims—most of them newly-weds—soon realize their folly, but by then it is too late. The hapless gents are transformed into look alikes of 'Gabbar Singh', the photographers even slinging a

---

[139]Hari Har Lal P., *The Doon Valley Down the Ages* (New Delhi: Interprint, 1993), 191.

bandolier (with plastic bullets) across the chest of their models to accompany the toy guns. Ladies are decked up like Sharmila Tagore in the movie, *Kashmir ki Kali*. After the ordeal is over, the zealous photographers promise to get the prints delivered at the hotel of the visitor, and believe me, they do keep their word.

Those fond of walking may avoid the ropeway and take a steep two kilometre long walk to the top from near the Kutchery on Mall Road.

The House without a Roof

No story about Mussoorie is complete without a ghost—when I recall such stories, I shudder to imagine if these ghosts are still lurking around the town. What if they are watching me write about them, reading every word I write and smiling when I miss some detail?

The tale of a house atop Gun Hill—the house whose roof was repeatedly blown away by wind; the house whose last inhabitant died mysteriously; the house abandoned for over four decades now—is one such haunting tale that still gives me goosebumps.

When friends in the waterworks told me about their guest house at Gun Hill where tin-roofs would not stay fixed, my first reaction was, 'The winds must be too strong, get a good carpenter to fix the roof securely.'

'It is not about the carpenter. It's not about the strong winds either. The house is haunted,' retorted Mr T; the details subsequently shared by him were sufficient to set me rushing up to Gun Hill.

As I pushed the wooden door of the ill-fated house, it creaked loudly in protest, startling me. My companions pulled at my sleeve, asking me to turn back.

'*Bhoot lag jayega tujhe* (the ghost will haunt you),' one of them shouted.

Despite their remonstrations, I managed to muster the

courage to enter the house. The putrid smell of decaying wood and dampness greeted my nostrils. The floor was lit with sunlight, and as I looked up to examine the roof, I could just see clear blue sky and a few wooden rafters. The wind howled through the decaying windows, as if in warning.

'Guest house' of waterworks department located at Gun Hill in 2014. Notice the missing roof.

Paint and plaster were peeling off the walls that had faced years of neglect. The floor was covered with a thick layer of dust. *When was the last time someone had set foot on this floor*, I wondered.

I felt very uncomfortable inside the house and, despite the bright sun, a chill went up my spine. As I rushed out of the house, the view of Mussoorie and the Doon Valley left me spellbound. *Nice location for a guest house, if only the unwanted guests were kept at bay*, I thought.

Mr Rawat, an elderly photographer at Gun Hill, informed that a watchman of waterworks stayed in this house in the 1970s. 'He often told us that he heard strange sounds. Often, he felt as if someone was hammering on the roof and frequently, sections of the tin roof were blown away. Occasional knocks on the door or rattling of windows was a common occurrence,' Mr Rawat narrated. 'The watchman was a brave, unflappable man. He was undeterred and attributed these events to the strong wind,' he said.

In 1978 the brave watchman was drowned after he fell into the water tank while putting chlorine in the tank to disinfect the water. By this time, a large crowd of shopkeepers had gathered to listen to this gory tale. 'The watchman's body was recovered from the tank several days later after much toil,' rose a voice from the crowd.

No wonder the waterworks department could not persuade any other watchman to stay at the guest house.

A few days later, I met the town's chronicler, Mr Gopal Bhardwaj, who reluctantly parted with some more details. 'The story dates back to 1920 when the tank was being built at Gun Hill,' Mr Bhardwaj said. 'Pathans from Afghanistan were hired as labourers and two of them got into a quarrel; it turned so nasty that one of them beheaded the other. Since then, sightings of a beheaded ghost have been reported,' he informed.

Was it the ghost of the Pathan that was haunting the guest house and blowing away the roof? Or was it just the strong wind? What about the strange noises heard by the watchman? Did he fall accidentally into the tank or did some invisible hand push him in?

Some things are best left unanswered.

Meanwhile, the last time the guest house was occupied was in 1982, when officials accompanying the then President Giani Zail Singh were housed here for one night. Hopefully, the Pathan's ghost did not make an appearance that night!

6

THE HIMALAYAN PARISHES

Nestled just above Mall Road near Gandhi Chowk, barely hidden from the eyes of bustling tourists, is the first church of the Himalayas. Indeed! The Christ Church of Mussoorie, with its awe-inspiring Gothic design, was the first church to come up in the Himalayas in the year 1839. The Queen of the Hills has eight such jewels in her crown that date back to the nineteenth century, hidden from prying eyes.

Casual visitors to the town—the weekend tourists—are in a rush to complete their tour by visiting waterfalls, the ropeway and other trivia, followed by a shopping spree on the Mall. For me, personally, the impressive designs of the churches, coupled with their rich history, make these places of worship a must visit.

A tree planted by the then Princess of Wales, who later became Queen Mary[140], still stands proudly in the compound of one of the churches. There's another church where the parents of the legendary hunter-turned-conservationist Jim Corbett tied the nuptial knot, and yet another where Hindi was taught since the late nineteenth century to Christian missionaries who arrived in India.

Christ Church (1839)

There is a fascinating bit of history involving the construction of the Christ Church. In April of 1836, when Reverend Daniel

---

[140]Mary of Teck (1867–1953) was the daughter of Duke of Teck. She was married to Prince George, the then Duke of York, in 1893. In 1901, Prince George was made the Prince of Wales and, in 1910, he was crowned the King-Emperor George V and Mary became Queen Mary.

Wilson[141] arrived in Mussoorie, there was no church in the town. 'Divine service was performed twice each Sunday at Landour, the sanatorium for sick soldiers.'[142]

Reverend Daniel persuaded the citizenry to build a church. Plans and possible sites were identified, and funds were raised. The cost of building the church was estimated to be ₹3,100, and a sum of ₹3,200 was raised.

The church was to be built on a high hill near Zephyr Hall (in the present-day Kulri area of the town) on the land of a Mr Whiting. '[...] Bateman, my Chaplain, had sketched an elevation for a church, fifty feet by twenty five, to hold two hundred people; and I had finished my letter to Mr Whiting, the owner of the land,' observed Reverend Daniel in his diary on 26 April 1836.[143]

A picture taken in the 1890s showing Christ Church (towards the left). (Picture courtesy: Hotel Savoy, Mussoorie)

---

[141]Reverend Daniel Wilson was the Bishop of Calcutta (now Kolkata) and first Metropolitan of India and Ceylon (Sri Lanka).

[142]Bateman J., *The Life of the Right Rev. Daniel Wilson, D.D., Vol. II* (London: John Murray, 1860), 107.

[143]Ibid, 108.

But fate had something else in store. John Mackinnon, an influential citizen and owner of the Mussoorie Seminary School on the far western spur of the town, objected to the location of the church.[144] He believed Zephyr Hall would be too far for his pupils, and the ideal location would be towards the west (present-day Gandhi Chowk) and was able to influence the residents.

Availability of land towards the west was explored, and Reverend Proby—a minister—agreed to donate a 'hundred feet by sixty feet'[145] plot out of his garden located above Mall Road overlooking the Doon Valley.

Finally, the foundation stone was laid for Christ Church on Saturday, 14 May 1836. It was a momentous day. Close to five hundred citizens gathered for the ceremony as Reverend Daniel laid the foundation stone. Colonel Young read a copy of the inscription, while the Gurkha regiment commanded by him played the national anthem after the ceremony.

'It will be the first church raised amidst the eternal snows of Upper India,'[146] wrote Reverend Daniel in his journal.

Captain Rennie Tailyour of Bengal Engineers supervised the construction of the tower and the main hall of the church[147] in 1836 (the chapel[148] and transepts[149] were added in 1853,[150] when L.D. Hearsey, son of the famous Hyder Jung Hearsey, presented the bell).

---

[144]Bodycot F., *Guide to Mussoorie* (Mussoorie: Mafasilite Printing Works, 1907), 32.

[145]Bateman J., *The Life of the Right Rev. Daniel Wilson, D.D., Vol. II* (London: John Murray, 1860), 108.

[146]Ibid, 109.

[147]Hari Har Lal P., *The Doon Valley Down the Ages* (New Delhi: Interprint, 1993), 187.

[148]Part of a church, near the altar.

[149]In a church, the transept is an area constructed perpendicular or crosswise to the main hall.

[150]Kinney T., *The Echo Guide to Mussoorie* (Mussoorie: Echo Press, 1908), 11.

A recent picture of the Christ Church building.

Three years later, Reverend Daniel visited the town again to consecrate the church, which 'was finished and looked beautiful'.[151]

Christ Church is an exquisite specimen of neo-Gothic architecture, with an elegant tower at the entrance bordered by four spires, windows with pointed arches and a main hall with transepts that give the church the shape of a cross. The pre-Raphaelite stained-glass windows, with their vast array of colours, depict the life of Jesus Christ and adorn this house of worship. It is believed that the Christ Church in Shimla, built in 1857, was modelled on the design of this church.

A pipe organ, manufactured by the famous William Hill[152] of England, was installed in the Christ Church in the 1870s. Played by the church's organist, Dorothy Hickie, for over forty years, the organ is non-functional since nearly half a century, but continues to be a proud possession of the church.

A deodar (*Cedrus deodara*) tree that stands tall in the courtyard

---

[151]Bateman J., *The Life of the Right Rev. Daniel Wilson, D.D., Vol. II* (London: John Murray, Albemarle-Street, 1860), 180.

[152]William Hill & Son was the most famous pipe organ manufacturing firm in England during the nineteenth century. This firm was established by William Hill and later joined by his sons, William and Thomas.

A deodar tree planted by Mary of Teck—the then Princess of Wales, who was later crowned Queen Mary in 1906—still stands tall in the church compound.

of the church is a reminder of another fascinating bit of history. This tree was planted on 4 March 1906 by Mary of Teck, the then Princess of Wales, who was later crowned Queen Mary. Mary visited Mussoorie along with her husband, George V, who ascended the throne of England in 1910. Incidentally, it was Mary who got the famous 'Crown of Queen Mary'[153] made for her, which was studded with the priceless Koh-i-Noor diamond that the British had acquired from Maharaja Ranjeet Singh.

Christ Church shot into national news when the correspondent of *The Statesman* wrote to his paper about a sermon being delivered there by Reverend Hackett on 22 October 1884. 'The Reverend gentleman discoursed upon the highly immoral tone of the society up here, that it far surpassed any other hill station in the scale of morals; that ladies and gentlemen after attending church proceeded to a drinking shop, a restaurant adjoining the library (the old 'Criterion') and there indulged freely in pegs, not one but many;

---

[153]The 'Crown of Queen Mary' was made for her in 1911. Apart from the Koh-i-Noor, this crown was also studded with 94.4 carat Cullinan III and 63.6 carat Cullinan IV—both parts of the famous 3106 carats 'Cullinan Diamond' that was found at Premier Mine in Cullinan, South Africa. After Mary's death in 1953, the crown has been kept at the Tower of London. 'Queen Mary's Crown 1911', *Royal Collection Trust*, https://www.rct.uk/collection/31704/queen-marys-crown

that at a fancy bazaar held this season, a lady stood up on a chair and offered her kisses to gentlemen at ₹5 each. What would they think of such society at home? But this was not all. Married ladies and married gents formed friendships and associations which tended to no good purpose, and set a bad example.'[154]

Christ Church was again in the middle of a storm in 1933 when the chaplain offered prayers for Motilal Nehru (father of Jawaharlal Nehru) during a Sunday service. Nehru, who had his summer abode in Mussoorie, was suffering from serious illness at that time. This did not go down well with the British, and the Reverend was severely reprimanded.

After running into disrepair for many decades, the Christ Church has been restored to its former glory. It is just a few minutes of an uphill walk from the Mall Road near Gandhi Chowk.

A postcard showing St. Paul's Church at Char Dukan in the 1890s.

---

[154]The Rambler, *A Mussoorie Miscellany* (Mussoorie: Mafasilite Press, 1936), 43–44.

St. Paul's Church (1840)

Mary Janet Prussia escaped the clutches of death as the Agra Fort was attacked by Indian freedom fighters during the Mutiny of 1857. Mary and her three children found safe haven in Mussoorie, but her husband was killed shortly thereafter in the battle at Etawah in Uttar Pradesh. Mary happened to meet Christopher William Corbett,[155] a British military officer posted at Mussoorie, and love blossomed. Christopher was a widower himself, and the duo got married in 1859.

This love story is quite significant as Christopher and Mary were the parents of the legendary hunter-turned-conservationist Jim Corbett (born in 1875), and the church where they tied the nuptials was St. Paul's Church at Char Dukan.

Consecrated on 1 May 1840,[156] St. Paul's was the second church to come up in the town and it is also neo-Gothic in design. Located at a height of over 7,000 feet, the beautiful church casts a spell upon the visitors. It has a grand entrance, with three large pointed arches with stone pillars, and the bell tower atop the roof adds to the charm.

St. Paul's was constructed to serve the British soldiers who were posted and recuperating in the Landour Cantonment. The walls of the church hall are adorned with plaques in the memory of the soldiers who died here, perhaps while seeking treatment at the 'convalescent depot' in the cantonment.

Another famous wedding at St. Paul's was that of Bollywood actor and Mussoorie resident Tom Alter in 1978. Recollecting the ceremony, Ajay Mark, a teacher at Woodstock School, once proudly told me that he was the best man at the wedding.

---

[155]Christopher William Corbett was a military officer posted at Landour who, subsequent to his marriage, left the military to join the postal service. He served as a postmaster at Landour Post Office for a few years before being transferred to Nainital in 1862.

[156]Kinney T., *The Echo Guide to Mussoorie* (Mussoorie: Echo Press, 1908), 11.

All Saint's Church (1840s)

Only the old timers are perhaps aware that All Saint's was the third church to come up in the town, sometime in the 1840s. It was built on the grounds of Castle Hill Estate[157] (now known as Survey Estate after its ownership was transferred to the Survey of India) in the Landour area of the town. Perched upon a ridge between Kulri and Lal Tibba, amidst dense oak forests, this church was constructed by Mr George Taylor, the then owner of Castle Hill Estate. For nearly a century, it was used predominantly by the civilian population of Landour. Proby Cautley, a noted British engineer who built the Ganga Canal and founded the Thompson College of Engineering at Roorkee (which is now IIT Roorkee), tied the nuptial knot with Frances Bacon at this church.

All Saint's was dismantled in 1948, and its material was shifted to the Hindustani Church. A small cottage, built subsequently on the plinth of the Church, remains a distant reminder of the past glory and sanctity of this place.

St. Peter's Church (1840s)

Located atop a hill in the centre of Landour Cantonment at an altitude of around 7,500 feet, St. Peter's Church is the highest church in Mussoorie. Established in the 1840s, it is amongst the earliest churches while also being the first Catholic church in the Queen of the Hills.

The most striking feature is the unique design of the church, which is modelled as per the Greco-Roman style—a refreshing change from the neo-Gothic and Victorian designs of other

---

[157]Ownership of this estate passed on to the Survey of India and their office continued to be functional here until the early 1990s. The Survey office was shifted from Mussoorie to Dehradun and since then this sprawling estate lies in a derelict state.

churches. The Corinthian columns at the entrance with a gable roof make the entrance resemble the famous Pantheon of Rome.

Post-independence, the service stopped and the church went into disrepair; it was reopened in 2007 and restored in 2009.

An 1895 picture of Methodist Church in Kulri. One can see the clocks on the Church tower, which were subsequently damaged in the earthquake of 1905. (Photographer: T.A. Rust)

Methodist Church (1885)

As a child, I would always gaze at the central tower of the Methodist Church, which had an old wind vane mounted on the top. 'How beautiful!' I would often exclaim as I passed the building just next door. Old timers informed me that the tower used to be even more splendid—with four clocks, one on each side, before the earthquake of 1905 took its toll.

Williams (1936), while writing about this incident, mentions that the damage to the tower and its clocks prompted 'a certain wit to burst into doggerel'[158]:

---

[158]The Rambler, *A Mussoorie Miscellany* (Mussoorie: Mafasilite Press, 1936), 46.

THE Kulri clock has had a shock
ENOUGH to knock it off its block
AND make it rock—ah!
HANHART and Bechtler[159] both have tried
To titivate its shocked inside,
So now they've called Fisher
THE watchmaker and undertak-er!

Constructed in 1835, the Methodist Church was first christened as Osborne Memorial Church in memory of Lily, the daughter of Reverend Dennis Osborne, who was the founder. The church may have been renamed, but memories of Lily are kept alive by an inscription reading, 'Our Lily', at the entrance.

Another plaque put up by the Survey of India on the church grounds—perhaps in the early twentieth century—mentions the height of the church as 2,003 metres (6,571 feet).

Many years ago, lights installed on this building by the government added to the charm of this impressive structure. But like many other government projects the lights have ceased to function due to lack of maintenance.

Union Church (1874)

Just a stone's throw away from the famous Picture Palace is the Union Church. Situated on a small hillock on the road leading towards Landour, the church building was constructed in 1874, on land purchased from the family of Charles Grant Jr, a powerful British politician who was also appointed the Baron[160] of Glenelg.

---

[159]Mr Hanhart and Bechtler were both proprietors of jewellery and watch repairing establishments.

[160]A baron or baronet is a holder of baronetcy—a hereditary title awarded by Britain's rulers. This practice was introduced around the fourteenth century. Baronets are given the prefix 'Sir' before their names. The title of 'Baron' is ranked higher than that of a 'Lord' or a 'Knight'.

The Grant family owned prime properties in Mussoorie, including the land on which the Methodist Church was built; their mansion in Mussoorie was called Glenelg.

Hindustani Church (around 1870)

'You must listen to the choir of the Hindustani Church. They are amazing! I want them to perform on a bigger stage one day,' Bollywood actor Mr Tom Alter, a resident of Mussoorie and a dear friend, once told me. And at the insistence of my friend, this amazing choir was given an opportunity to perform at the Winterline Carnival in 2014 before a large audience—and they were absolutely stunning! No one was more pleased than my friend sitting alongside me in the audience. In fact, the Alter family has a long association with this church and has been supporting it in various ways.

This church was established in the mid-1870s to serve the Indian Christian population of Landour, primarily the families of the staff working in Woodstock School and hence the name: Hindustani Church. A most unique feature of this church is that the service is held in Hindi. The church is located inside the Woodstock campus and its current building was constructed in 1956.

Kellogg's Church (1903)

Dr Samuel H. Kellogg was a Canadian missionary theologist and linguist who dedicated his life teaching Hindi to Christian missionaries in the second half of the nineteenth century. Kellogg is regarded as the founder of the Landour Language School, which during the twentieth century became immensely popular with foreign students, academicians, aid-workers and others interested in learning Hindi. Kellogg had lost his life after a tragic fall in Landour, and the Kellogg Memorial Church was erected in his memory in 1903 in the premises of his school—a short distance above Char Dukan.

Kellogg Memorial, Landour, Mussoorie

A postcard showing the Kellogg Memorial Church in Landour Cantonment. (Photo courtesy: Hotel Savoy, Mussoorie)

7

GARDENS OF REMEMBRANCE

As this hill station took birth, it became a chosen destination for European immigrants who sought refuge here to escape the sultry heat of the plains. Many built their lodgings here, and several others established their businesses. The Redcoats too expectantly waited for the slightest opportunity to be sent to the 'Convalescent Depot' at Landour to get a few months of respite from the heat, mosquitoes and ongoing conflicts in the Indian plains.

The heat of the plains, along with rampant malaria, typhoid, dysentery, cholera, plague and tuberculosis took their toll upon the European settlers. The average age of death during the early colonial period was 'well under 30 for men and 25 for women'.[161]

Many sick and suffering civilians, as well as soldiers, reached Mussoorie hoping that the mountain air would help them recuperate. The visitors would stay in the hills for six to eight months before returning to the plains during the winters. But there were some who could never return. English, Irish, Scottish, German and some Italian immigrants too were laid to rest amidst these picturesque surroundings. They rest eternally in the cemeteries at Landour and Camel's Back Road to forever enjoy a climate much similar to their homes.

First Burial

The first burial was that of Sir Charles Farrington. Sir Charles was, in fact, a baron—being the second Baronet of the Farrington

---

[161]Wilkinson T., *Two Monsoons* (London: Gerald Duckworth and Co. Ltd., 1976), 6.

Baronetcy,[162] which was created in honour of distinguished military services of his grandfather. He was also a distinguished soldier—a Captain in the 31st Regiment, who had participated in the Battle of Talavera[163] at the age of fifteen, and also in the famous Battle of Waterloo[164] against the forces of Napoleon Bonaparte.

But alas! Sir Charles was not interred in any cemetery. God chose the roadside in Jharipani as his final resting place.

The grave of Sir Charles Farrington at Jharipani. The grave is now with in the campus of Oak Grove School.

---

[162]Farrington Baronetcy in the County of Kent in England was created in 1818 for General Sir Anthony Farrngton. After his death, Sir Charles inherited the baronetcy in 1823. 'Whitehall 3 October 1818', *The Gazette*, No. 17404, 1767, https://www.thegazette.cc.uk/London/issue/17404/page/1767

[163]The Battle of Talavera was fought in 1809 by a British–Spanish army against French-occupied Madrid

[164]The Battle of Waterloo was fought at Waterloo in Belgium in 1815. British-led allied forces defeated the French army under the command of Napoleon Bonaparte.

Suffering from tuberculosis (consumption as it was called in those days), Sir Charles was on his way to Landour[165]—hoping that a change of climate would help him recoup—but died enroute at Jharipani on 26 March 1828. Incidentally, Captain Mundy, a soldier who also wrote a travelogue, happened to pass this place on 15 April 1828—barely a fortnight after the death of Sir Charles. Mundy wrote about the grave in his journal: 'On a narrow but elevated platform of earth on the right of the road, we passed the new made grave of Sir Charles Farrington, of the thirty-first regiment who died of consumption on his way to Llandowr, whither he was repairing as a last hope, about a fortnight ago.' [166]

An obelisk was put on the grave shortly after, but Williams C. (1936) reported nearly a century later that '[...] obelisk has now not only been rebuilt, but has now been moved into the Oak Grove School's estate.'[167]

The reason I am writing about this grave at such length is because of some really strange events that are believed to be connected with this grave and Oak Grove School. Residents of Jharipani told me that in 1988 there was a landslide, and the grave, which had been relocated to a ridge (within the campus of Oak Grove School) above the old bridle path, came crashing down on the road. Immediately afterwards, some unfortunate events occurred at Oak Grove—their ambulance met with an accident and, shortly after, a student died.

School authorities felt that the grave of Sir Charles was a 'good luck charm' for the school. The grave was promptly restored, and there has been no incidence since.

'The grave of Sir Charles atop this ridge overlooking the Doon

---

[165]The 'Convalescent Depot' or the 'Invalid Establishment' was not operational until April 1829, but since 1828, sick soldiers had begun to arrive at the station.
[166]Mundy G.C., *Pen and Pencil Sketches, Being the Journal of a Tour in India: Vol I* (London: John Murray, Albemarle-Street, 1858), 187.
[167]The Rambler, *A Mussoorie Miscellany* (Mussoorie: Mafasilite Press, 1936), 110.

Valley is a good luck charm for the school as well as all residents of Jharipani. Sir Charles is protecting and guarding all of us from harm,' a Jharipani shopkeeper earnestly remarked as I went to take pictures of the grave.

Maybe the residents are right—the old soldier is still lurking around, keeping a vigil on Jharipani!

Landour Cemetery

The roadside burial of Sir Charles sent alarm bells ringing, and the cantonment authorities immediately set out to find burial space—especially since the sick soldiers, like Sir Charles, had been arriving in Landour, albeit in limited numbers. By the end of spring, space for a cemetery was designated on the 'Landour Mall' or 'Upper Chakkar'—a road that presently goes beyond Char Dukan, passes Lal Tibba and comes out at present-day Language School (see chapter 2). Terraces were developed amidst dense deodar trees and Protestant and Roman Catholic cemeteries were established.

A timely move indeed, as soon thereafter Captain George Bolton, of the 2nd European Regiment, came to need his final resting place. He was buried at the Landour Cemetery on 13 June 1828.

Also resting here are thirteen soldiers who had been a part of World War I—the injured soldiers came to recoup at the Convalescent or Invalids Depot at Landour, but unfortunately ended up in the cemetery. Among them is a lieutenant, several lance corporals, a gunner, a rifleman and a few privates.

A 2013 picture of Tom Alter and Benjamin Gilani during the shoot of Ek Fursat-e-Gunah at Landour Cemetery.

In 2013, I got a sudden message from Tom Alter saheb. 'I am shooting in the Landour Cemetery. Please come and meet me this afternoon,' the message said.

I learnt that Tom saheb was shooting for his serial, *Ek Fursat-e-Gunah,* in the cemetery. One could never refuse Tom saheb, so I reached promptly after lunch, only to find him being 'held at gunpoint' by Benjamin Gilani saheb.

After the shoot, he took me for a walk in the cemetery, also showing me the graves of his ancestors buried on the terrace just above the road.

I observed the thirteen graves of soldiers of World War I to be conspicuously different and well-maintained.

'Sir, these graves don't look very old. But the gravestones mention the date of burial between 1916 and 1920' I said.

'These are maintained by the Commonwealth War Graves Commission. They were renovated recently,' the actor explained.

As we came to the gate of the cemetery, a tall deodar tree caught my eye.

'This was planted in 1870—nearly 150 years ago—by the Duke of Edinburgh. Read the plaque attached to the tree,' Tom saheb told me.

I found out later that in March 1906, during her visit to Mussoorie, the then Princess of Wales[168] had also visited the Landour Cemetery.

'Landour was covered with more than a foot of snow, and some of the roads were impassable. However, a path was dug to the cemetery where the tree planted by the Duke of Edinburgh was seen to be flourishing exceedingly,'[169] mentions a journal narrating the then princess's tour to India.

Perhaps this tree inspired the princess to plant one herself at Christ Church two days later on 4 March 1906.

---

[168]Later to become the Queen of The United Kingdom.

[169]Reed S., *The Royal Tour in India* (Bombay: Bennett Coleman & Co., 1906), 412.

Roman Catholic Cemetery in Landour

Roman Catholic Cemetery, Landour.

Most people are only aware about one cemetery in Landour, i.e. the Landour Cemetery. But actually, two cemeteries were established in Landour. John Northam's journal (1884)[170] mentions that the Landour Mall passed between the two cemeteries with Protestant Cemetery (known today as the Landour Cemetery) above the road and the Roman Catholic Cemetery below the road. Both the cemeteries were consecrated in 1840 by Daniel Wilson, the then Bishop of Calcutta.

Unfortunately, not many people are aware about the existence of the Roman Catholic Cemetery, which is located below the 'Landour Mall' or 'Upper Chakkar' and one needs to peep down the edge of the road to see the graves amidst a dense thicket of trees.

There is not much information about the people buried in this cemetery, but I did find that during World War II, Italian

---

[170]Northam J., *Guide to Masuri, Landaur, Dehradun and The Hills North of Dehra* (Calcutta: Thacker, Spink and Co., 1884), 62.

prisoners-of-war had been held captive in Dehradun,[171] and some of them who fell sick were sent off to Mussoorie to recuperate. The unfortunate ones, who passed away at Mussoorie, were laid to rest in this cemetery. The graves of these men and women are crudely made—shaped like an inverted cone with a base of common stone and slate—after all, they were 'prisoners of war'. But I hope that these unfortunate souls have found peace here in this 'alien' territory.

Camel's Back Cemetery

The master storyteller, Ruskin Bond, has a unique way of surprising people. One day, while we were on a call, he startled me

The lychgate of Camel's Back Cemetery.

by announcing that the grave of James Bond is in Camel's Back Cemetery.

'Wasn't James Bond a fictional character in Ian Fleming's novels? How is this possible?' I blurted. I sensed the great man smiling mischievously.

'The story goes like this,' he said. 'I used to explore the Camel's Back Cemetery and look for interesting graves. I found a gravestone which bore the name James Bond. Sometime later, at a literary fest, someone joked, "Are you related to James Bond?" to which I nodded and added, "He is buried in the Camel's Back Cemetery in Mussoorie."'

---

[171]A prisoners-of-war camp was established at present-day Clement Town in Dehradun. Prisoners were primarily Italians—including troops captured in North Africa and the families of Italians incarcerated in India—who were brought here during World War II. Clement Town was named after Father R.C. Clement, an Italian priest who had settled here in 1931.

The great man chuckled and both of us had a hearty laugh. Ruskin Sir also told me that after finding the grave, he had checked the burial register and had found that the James Bond buried in the cemetery was a dentist who had worked with the Survey of India. So he coined a verse about the dentist, which goes:

'Stranger walk with gravity,
The dentist is filling his last cavity.'[172]

Later, upon browsing through the burial records, I found that Mr James Bond was buried in the cemetery in February 1924.

Some other interesting names cropped up from the burial records:

Henry Moorhouse Bohle (d.1851), liquor baron, who had set up the town's first brewery and who remained at loggerheads with Captain Young—the founding father of Mussoorie.

Australian barrister and author John Lang (d.1864), who had contested a lawsuit on behalf of Rani Lakshmibai opposing the annexation of Jhansi to the British under the 'Doctrine of Lapse'. Lang started a newspaper in 1845 called *The Mofussilite*,[173] which often took a critical line against the East India Company. '*The Mofussilite*, when edited by its founder, John Lang, attained a very high position in India's newspaper literature.'[174] John Lang wrote several novels, including, *The Forger's Wife* (1855), which, literary experts believe, was among the earliest detective novels in the English language. He was among a distinguished group of authors to contribute to *Household Words*, an English weekly magazine edited by Charles Dickens.

Lang's grave went into oblivion and lay neglected for decades until Ruskin Bond rediscovered it and placed a marker on it in

---

[172]Personal conversation with me.
[173]Mofussilite means one who lives in a small town.
[174]Laurie W.F.B., *Sketches of Some Distinguished Anglo-Indians with an Account of Anglo-Indian Periodical Literature* (London: W.H. Allen & Co, 1887), 350.

1992. It said, 'A tribute from one author to another.'

Also resting here is John A. Hindmarsh (d.1890) who, along with 600-odd British soldiers, was immortalized in 1854 during the Crimean War. Misinterpretation of an order led to these brave cavalrymen charging head-on into booming Russian guns at the battle of Balaklava. The assault ended with high British casualties.

Few months later, Alfred Tennyson commemorated these braves through his poem 'The Charge of the Light Brigade'. Thirty-six years later, Nobel Laureate Rudyard Kipling also wrote a poem, 'The Last of the Light Brigade', which was about the terrible hardship faced in old age by the survivors of the Crimean War.

Hindmarsh was amongst the few hundred men who had survived the charge. How and when he had arrived in Mussoorie? Had he retired? Was he recuperating? These are some questions buried in the sands of time.

The maverick business tycoon Frederick aka 'Pahari' Wilson (d.1883) and his wife Gulabi aka 'Ruth' Wilson made a fortune cutting trees from Garhwal mountains and floating them to the plains via the Ganga and Yamuna rivers. Wilson owned considerable property in Mussoorie and Dehradun.

Apart from logging timber, it seems another interest of Wilson lay in the works of the author Sir Walter Scott. Two of his properties in Mussoorie were named after the works of Scott: Rokeby—after an 1813 poem; and Ivanhoe—after an 1819 novel. There is much more about Wilson—to be revealed sometime later.

Jews were also laid to rest at Camel's Back Cemetery. Resting here is Mr Saul Hakman—a renowned hairdresser who later established the iconic 'Hakman's Hotel' on the Mall. Mr Hakman died due to a brain haemorrhage in 1932, aged 51.

During the 1970s through the 1990s, a large number of graves were vandalized at Camel's Back Cemetery. 'Most of the headstones on the graves were made with the "carrara"[175] marble imported

---

[175]Carrara marble is a white or blue-grey marble that is obtained from the mountains near the town of Carrara in Italy. This marble has been quarried

from Italy. High market value of this marble probably made the kabadi-wallahs steal the headstones,' says Mr Hugh Gantzer.

Be it the kabadi-wallahs who did this for monetary gains or local lads who did it just for fun, the damage was irreparable.

Due to its close proximity to the Mall, this cemetery was also thronged by tourists. It also became a rendezvous point for young couples. Unfortunately, there was no fencing or barricades in those days to prevent unauthorized entry into the cemetery.

I know of several people in the town who, as teenagers, hooked up with girls on the Mall or at the Rink, and then came to the cemetery to take advantage of the solitude. I won't say more!

Thankfully, the cemetery committee, led by Mr Hugh Gantzer, put an end to this: 'I wrote to the chief of the Indian Army, apprising him about the number of graves of soldiers in the cemetery and the need to protect the graves from vandalism,' Mr Gantzer said. One fine day, he received a phone call from the sub-area headquarters informing him that the army had sanctioned funds to build a wall around the cemetery.

This is how a wall was built, and a plaque was also installed inside the lychgate to thank the Indian army. A fence was added on top of the wall after the local MLA, acting upon the request of Mr Gantzer, provided funds for the fence.

I'm sure this has put an end to the disturbance in the cemetery, and that the dead are now able to rest in peace!

Murders and Suicides in Mussoorie

Browsing through the burial register of Camel's Back Cemetery, pneumonia, tuberculosis and heart failure appeared to be the most common causes of death during the nineteenth and early twentieth century. But gory incidents did happen, even in this tranquil and 'safe' town.

---

since Roman times and is much preferred for use in monuments or sculptures.

A tombstone dating back to 1909 at Camel's Back Cemetery bears the awful words: 'Murdered by the hands that he befriended.' This is the final resting place of James Reginal Clapp, who worked as an assistant at the chemist shop of Messrs J.B. & E. Samuel. Corporal Allen, his friend, who was later sentenced to death for the murder of Clapp, was accused of stealing money from Clapp and murdering him. Allen, who was apprehended at Rajpur, vehemently protested his innocence.

'I was in the company of a woman the night this crime was committed. I am innocent,' Allen is believed to have repeatedly said.

But Allen refused to utter the name of the woman.

'I cannot besmirch the reputation of that lady,' he is believed to have said.

'Then off to the gallows you go,' pronounced the magistrate.

Finally, Allen was hanged at Nainital Jail—labelled a 'murderer' and a 'backstabber'.

But was he really guilty? Why was the money he was accused of robbing from Mr Clapp never found? Was he really in the company of some woman that night? Why did he not disclose the name of the woman? Why did the woman not come forth to protect her paramour? All these questions will remain unanswered.

Another love affair resulted in a tragic end in the year 1917, when 14-year-old Herbert fell in love. But this young cupid-smitten boy failed to realize that his 'lady-love' was a woman much older than him. Finally, when he was spurned by the woman, the heartbroken lad ended his life.

In the same year, two persons of a family succumbed to 'gunshot wounds' on the same day. These unfortunate events transpired with the Fenemores. It so happened that Millicent Fenemore, a teacher, somehow got entangled in a defamation suit that was being heard at the court. Each hearing of the suit disturbed the husband, Stephen (also a teacher), who was apparently concerned about the family's honour. Finally (on 24

November 1917) Stephen decided to take the extreme step. When Millicent was sound asleep, Stephen crept to her bedside and shot her in the head with a revolver. Subsequently, Stephen—who was a captain in the Mussoorie Volunteer Rifles—shot himself with his rifle; both were buried in Camel's Back Cemetery on 25 November.

Another tragedy occurred on 25 July 1927. This time, the victim was 53-year-old Mrs Anna Amelia Owen, wife of Mr Percy Owen. It was revealed to me that the Owens ran a boarding house somewhere in Kulri. One fateful afternoon, in a fit of rage, Mr Owen shot his wife, wounded his daughter Helen and then shot himself. Luckily, Basil, their teenage son, was not in the house when this incident occurred.

'But if Mr and Mrs Owen both died, why is there a record of the burial of only Mrs Owen?' I wondered.

The truth dawned on me several years later, when an old timer enlightened me that as per his last wish, Mr Owen was cremated; hence his name does not find a mention in the burial register. A Christian wished a cremation! Strange, isn't it?

8

PLEASURE CAPITAL OF THE RAJ

I had a little husband
Who gave me all his pay.
I left him for Mussoorie
A hundred miles away.
I dragged my little husband's name
Through heaps of social mire.
And joined him in November
As good as you'd desire.[176]

Come summer, wives of European officers and civil servants deployed in India's plains would promptly pack their bags, bid adieu to their husbands and rush off to the cool hills. These were the 'grass-widows' of the Raj era—a somewhat demeaning title given to wives who spent summers in hills while their husbands remained on duty in the plains.[177] Along with the grass widows, hordes of unmarried females, widows and spinsters also joined the bandwagon.

Close on the heels of these females were the numerous Tommies[178]—young and middle aged—most of whom would feign sick-leave and spend their summers in 'fair' company. Their guiding star was often the station master at Dehradun who kept a watchful eye on all arrivals and would often send

---

[176]Wright G., *Hill Stations of India* (Hong Kong: Odyssey, 1991), 26.

[177]Yule H. & Burnell A.C., *Hobson–Jobson: A Dictionary of Colloquial Anglo-Indian Words and Phrases, and of Kindered Terms, Etymological, Historical, Geographical and Discursive* (London: John Murray, 1903), 394.

[178]Tommy is a colloquial term used to refer to private soldiers in the British Army.

the 'Jacks' up the hill to meet the 'Jills'.[179]

And then there were the 'conservative' married women—accompanied by their husbands and children—who would scorn on their counterparts who came here to let their hair down. These conservatives derived their share of fun from gossip mongering at tea parties.

All and sundry were welcome to the 'Pleasure Capital of the Raj'!

Readers might be wondering that they heard of Shimla as the summer capital of the British; Nainital as the summer capital of the United Provinces; and Darjeeling as the summer capital of the Bengal Presidency; but never ever heard of a 'pleasure capital'.

Dear readers, for all practical purposes, Mussoorie was the official or unofficial 'pleasure capital' of the British in India. A well-earned name that the queen lived up to, even after India's independence.

WINTERGARDEN
S A V O Y
Phone 10   Phone 10

THIS WEEK

Monday 4th	LATE DANCE & CABARET	From 8 p.m. Admission Rs. 1/5
Tuesday 5th Admission Free	COCKTAIL DANCE & CABARET	From 7-30 p.m.
Thursday 7th Admission Free	COCKTAIL DANCE & CABARET	From 7-30 p.m.
Saturday 9th	LATE DANCE & CABARET	From 8 p.m. Admission Rs. 1/5

FULL PROGRAMME OF CABARET NUMBERS
By
**XENIA ZARINA, RONALD & ANGELA
DIMITRI, KSENIA, PAM & HONEY**
Music By
BORIS and his BAND
DINNER and SOUPER A LA CARTE-SERVED In The BALLROOM

Hotel Savoy advertisement about cocktails and cabarets featuring European artists. (Source: The Mussoorie Advertiser, 9 June 1947, Vol. 5, No. 8, Mussoorie: Mussoorie Art Press)

A sanatorium that became the 'pleasure capital'

Mussoorie was never meant to be the pleasure capital; it was built as a sanatorium where British soldiers could rest and recuperate. As the ailing soldiers started pouring in, some were accompanied by their wives, who pretty much enjoyed the congenial climate.

---

[179]The Rambler, *A Mussoorie Miscellany* (Mussoorie: Mafasilite Press, 1936), 109.

Another aspect that worked in Mussoorie's favour was the social bonhomie and seclusion it provided while the weather resembled that of Britain.

Fanny Parks—a travel writer from Isle of Wight who came to these parts in the early half of nineteenth century—wrote, 'How delicious is this coldness in the Hills! —it is just as wet, windy, and wretched as in England.'[180]

A postcard showing the Mall Road (circa 1925). The Mall was a happening place—notice the men and women on horseback, people pulling a rickshaw can also be seen. Exchange Building (now Hotel Clarks) is visible in the background while the wooden staircase on the left led to the iconic Kwality restaurant.

Soon enough, it became a tradition for the bored and heat-scorched wives of officers to rush to the hills during the summers. Sure, there were women who also visited with their husbands and children, but the Mussoorie summer show, so to say, was for those looking to get away from both the heat and husbands.

---

[180]Parks F., *Wanderings of a Pilgrim in Search of the Picturesque: Vol. II* (London: Pelham Richardson, 1850), 239.

While there was no dearth of scenic hill stations in India to provide a temporary fix for British homesickness, Mussoorie was different. Unlike Shimla (called 'Simla' during the British Raj) or Darjeeling, there were no officers strutting about, and no frequent official business.

According to acclaimed travel writer Mr Hugh Gantzer, the British kept Mussoorie deliberately free from 'officialdom' and summer capital starchiness to provide an opportunity to the young bucks for some revelry.[181]

Mussoorie became like the back bench of a classroom, away from the glare of the teacher, where students are left to their own devices. Without the constraints imposed by the imperial order in the plains, the young officers who came here on leave were inclined to let loose, and the grass-widows too looked forward to some fun.

The town had a somewhat surreal and frivolous atmosphere due to the presence of adventurous men and women. The vacationers kept themselves engaged in a series of lunches, dinners, fancy dress

---

FRIDAY 8th August

SAVOY—phone 10

HAKMAN'S—Long Cocktail Dance
6-30 to 11 p.m.
STANDARD—Lucky Table Night
6 to 10-30 p.m.

MAJESTIC—Les Miserables
2-30, 6 & 9-30
CAPITOL—Gone with the Wind
2-29, 6 & 9-30
RIALTO—Cleopatra
2-30, 6 & 9-30
P. Palace—phone 55

SATURDAY 9th August

SAVOY—Late Dance & Cabaret
8 p.m. to ???
HAKMAN'S—Winter Sports in St. Moritz
8 p.m. till ???

STANDARD—Late Dance
8 p.m. till ?

MAJESTIC—Les Miserables
2-30, 6 & 9-30
CAPITOL—Gone with the Wind
2-30, 6 & 9-30
RIALTO—Sudan
2-30, 6 & 9-30
P. Palace—phone 55

SUNDAY 10th August

SAVOY—phone 10

HAKMAN'S—Long Cocktail Dance
6-30 till 11-30 p.m.
STANDARD—Tea Dance & Cabaret
7-30 to 10 p.m.
MAJESTIC—phone 105
2-30, 6 & 9-30
CAPITOL—Monsieur Beaucaire
2-30, 6 & 9-30
RIALTO—Sudan
2-30, 6 & 9-30
P. Palace—phone 55

Visitors to Mussoorie were kept busy and had much to choose from—as indicated by a schedule of upcoming dances, cabarets at Savoy, Hakman's and Standard in August 1947. Notice that on Saturday the programmes commenced at 8 p.m. but the time of ending is denoted by question marks (???) indicating all night revelry and partying. Also given are the timings of movie shows at Majestic, Capitol and Rialto. (Source: The Mussoorie Advertiser, 4 August 1947, Vol. 5, No. 16, Mussoorie: Mussoorie Art Press)

---

[181]Personal conversation with me.

parties, tea parties, picnics, balls, social calls, fetes or even horse rides and walks on the Mall and Camel's Back. But these 'seemingly innocent' engagements were just the tip of the iceberg. The grass widows were accused of 'licentious behaviour'[182] perhaps tempted by the presence of many young and fun-seeking officers.[183]

A fancy dress ball at Hotel Savoy with men and women dressed as Egyptians. (Picture courtesy: Hotel Savoy, Mussoorie)

Mrs Robert Moss King—who has published her diary on her travels in India—reached Mussoorie in the autumn of 1878. During her first dinner at a hotel here she disapproved of the ladies present at the dining table and observed '[…] a few ladies (save the mark!) looking and behaving as much like barmaids as they could.'[184]

---

[182]Kennedy D., *Magic Mountains: Hills Stations and the British Raj* (Berkeley: University of California Press, 1996), 126.
[183]Ibid.
[184]King R.M., *The Diary of a Civilians Wife in India: 1877–1882; Vol I* (London: Richard Bentley and Sons, 1884), 141.

HAKMAN'S

SATURDAY 14TH JUNE 1947
8 p.m. to 2 a.m.

CIRCUS NIGHT

THE GREATEST SHOW OF THE SEASON

CLOWNS - LEOPARDS
HORSES - DOGS - SNAKES
Acrobats - Magicians

UNDER THE PERSONAL CONTROL OF

JEANNE CARROL
(RING MASTER & TAMER)

WALLACES - DARLEYS - GRETA - GOGIA PASHA

AND

RITA THE SINGING DOG

Dont Miss this Outstanding Show
of the season

A June 1947 advertisement of a 'Circus Night' at Hakman's featuring clowns, acrobats and magicians. The magic show was by legendary Gogia Pasha. The timing was from 8 p.m. to 2 a.m. (Source: The Mussoorie Advertiser, 9 June 1947, Vol. 5, No. 8, Mussoorie: Mussoorie Art Press)

Meanwhile, the young privates felt emboldened to freely engage in 'poodle-faking'[185] with these ladies—something that was frowned upon by colonels of some regiments. 'Still, hill stations filled with

---

[185]Poodle-faking is a reproachful slang used in the British army for young officers who are found to be over-attentive to women.

bored wives whose husbands were sweating with their regiments on the plains below presented some officers on duty or leave there with a combination of desire and availability they found irresistible.'[186]

The Mall was the place for flirtations while the Camel's Back Road was chosen for secret rendezvous!

Every evening, the Mall was crowded with visitors—some on horseback or ponies, few on jhampans and most on foot. 'A gayer scene it would be impossible to conceive.'[187] Everything began at the Mall—it was 'the' place for exchanging pleasantries, sharing gossip, ogling, making passes and flirting.

A circa 1905 view of Mall Road from the Criterion restaurant. Operated by the owners of Charleville, Criterion was the post popular restaurant-cum-bar and a hub for social gatherings where the gentry gathered in the evening as the band played at Gandhi Chowk.

The local breweries produced enough beer to wet everyone's whistle—and maybe much more. The revelry also led to many

---

[186]Farwell B., *Armies of the Raj* (New York: W.W. Norton & Company, 1989), 140.

[187]Lang J., *The Mahommedan Mother* in Dickens C. (ed.), *Household Words: Vol. VII, Magazine No. 168*, 11 June 1853, 339.

romantic and amorous associations. The Scandal Point,[188] located at Camel's Back Road, was the preferred rendezvous for love birds—perhaps owing to its picturesque view and its secluded location.

Unsurprisingly, The Savoy had to invent the 'separation bell' to spare the blushes and avoid scandals. 'There is a hotel in Mussoorie where they ring a bell just before dawn so that the pious may say their prayers and impious get back to their own beds,'[189] observed Lovell Thomas (1926). As a measure of extra precaution, a superannuated, shortsighted concierge was entrusted with the task of ringing the bell. But scandals did happen! Elopements were reported as way back as in 1850s.

THE GAME!

An old-timer once remarked, 'Boy you have spent so much time on research, I'm sure you knew about "The Game".'

'The Game! What game, uncle?' I asked innocently.

'If you really have no knowledge about "The Game" then you know nothing about Mussoorie!' he mocked. Then he said that his father had heard tales of a somewhat erotic game being played by men and women.

He narrated that several women would sit around a large table while, turn by turn, men—obviously, those who were part of the same social circle—would be brought to the room blindfolded. The women would lift their skirts upto their knees while each man would crawl under the table (blindfold removed) and feel the uncovered legs of each woman in a bid to identify the women.

'I bet none of the men would ever have recognized any of the women,' I retorted.

'No, my boy, they did and quite frequently so!' he replied.

'And this game was right at the top of popularity charts!' the old timer exclaimed.

---

[188]See chapter 5 on Camel's Back Road.
[189]Thomas L., *India: Land of the Black Pagoda* (London: Hutchinson & Co, 1931), 220.

'There were two elopements. Mrs Merrydale went off with
Lieutenant Maxwell, leaving her children under the care of the
servants until her husband came to take them away. Mrs Hastings,
who used to bore us about the duties of a wife, carried off that
silly boy Stammersleigh,' writes John Lang.[190]

On occasions, when the scandals leaked, the enraged husbands
took cudgels against the revelling young Turks. As Byron Farwell
observes, 'Every season had its scandals, and it was said that
some poodle fakers came down from the hills fighting rearguard
actions against enraged husbands.'[191]

What could be more reckless than a woman auctioning their
kisses in public? Yes, such incidents were reported twice.

In 1884, the Reverend at Christ Church admonished the citizenry
and mentioned, 'At a fancy bazaar held this season, a lady stood up
on a chair and offered her kisses to gentlemen at ₹5 each.' Years later,
at a charity show in 1932, a lady auctioned a single kiss, for which
a gentleman paid ₹300.[192]

The pleasant climate and carefree society also attracted the
Indian royalty. Princely houses of Baroda, Jaipur, Jind, Kapurthala,
Kalsia, Nabha, Patiala and also the Nawab of Rampur built their
summer abodes here. These royals also had their share of fun—
with the Maharaja of Kapurthala, Jagatjit Singh, leading the way.

He threw dinner parties and receptions at Chateau de
Kapurthala, which were hugely popular and were attended by
Indian kings and princes as well as by British officers. Dance cards
were issued, on which the ladies made reservations for dances
but, on many occasions, couples would disappear into the park
and miss their dancing reservations.[193]

[190]Lang J., *The Himalaya Club* in Dickens C. (ed.), *Household Words: Vol. XV,*
Magazine No. 365, 21 March 1857, 271.
[191]Farwell B., *Armies of the Raj* (New York: W.W. Norton & Company, 1989), 140.
[192]Hari Har Lal P., *The Doon Valley Down the Ages* (New Delhi: Interprint, 1993), 219.
[193]Dass D.J. & Dass R.B., *Maharani* (Delhi: Hind Pocket Books Pvt. Ltd., 1973), 16.

An early twentieth century picture of Chateau de Kapurthala (extreme left), the summer palace of Jagatjit Singh, Maharaja of Kapurthala. The maharaja was famous for organizing lavish dinner parties and receptions at his palace that were attended by Indian royalty and British officers. The building of Hotel Savoy is also visible towards the right.

The highlight of each season was a 'virility contest', organized by a maharaja (not naming him). In this unique contest who's who of Indian royalty participated, and almost each year this contest was won by a royal from Punjab.[194]

Mujras were frequently organized for the royalty, and the Nawab of Rampur is believed to be especially fond of them.

Even the royals became unruly after a drink too many—the most famous incident being when a certain 'crown prince'[195] had to be evicted from Stiffle's restaurant on the Mall after he created a ruckus.

---

[194]I am not naming both of them lest their families feel offended.
[195]I am not naming him lest his family feels offended.

9

THE HALLS OF IVY

'It may be remarked, however, that Masuri is fast becoming one vast seminary, and may be termed as Edinburgh of India.'[196]

—John Northam

The history of Mussoorie's schools dates back to the first half of the nineteenth century when the first school was established in 1834. Subsequently, numerous schools emerged on the scene, many of whom are still thriving while many have closed down.

The development of Mussoorie on scholastic lines stemmed from the demand from European and Anglo-Indian civil servants and military officers serving in India, who did not or could not send their wards to England for education.

John Mackinnon, son-in-law of brewer Henry Bohle, set up the Masuri Seminary, which was perhaps the first school to be established in the Himalayas. This school was set up on the site of the 'old brewery' of Bohle. The school did pretty well until Mackinnon decided to shift to the brewery business, and Henry Ramsay took up the reins of the school for a short while; he did not meet with success and the seminary was temporarily closed in 1850.

Sensing that there was a good opening for setting up a school at Mussoorie, Reverend William Maddock, chaplain of Christ Church, called his brother Reverend Robert Maddock all the way from England. Masuri Seminary was relocated on the hill just behind the Mussoorie Library—where The Savoy Hotel is

---

[196]Northam J., *Guide to Masuri, Landaur, Dehradun and The Hills North of Dehra* (Calcutta: Thacker, Spink and Co., 1884), 61.

now—and came to be known as Maddock's School.[197] In 1865, this school was purchased by the Diocesan Board of Education with Reverend A.O. Hardy as the principal, who was later succeeded by Reverend Arthur Stokes, at which point this school came to be known as Stoke's School. The school was finally winded up in 1900 and, a few years later, The Savoy Hotel replaced the school.

Masuri Seminary School (also known as Maddock's School and Stoke's School) in 1860. After this school closed down it was replaced by The Savoy Hotel in 1902. Also seen in the background is the Christ Church. (Picture courtesy: Hotel Savoy, Mussoorie)

Apart from these, several other schools came up in the town in the nineteenth and early twentieth century, which included Convent of Jesus and Mary, Waverley, founded in 1845; St. George's College in 1853; Woodstock in 1854 (although it started as the Protestant Girls' School); Caineville School in 1865; St. Fidelis School and Military Orphanage in 1866; Summer Home for Soldiers' Children in 1876; Scinde, Punjab and Delhi Railway

---

[197]The Rambler, *A Mussoorie Miscellany* (Mussoorie: Mafasilite Press, 1936), 58.

School in 1877; Wynberg Allen School in 1888; Oak Grove School in 1888; Miss Holland's School in 1895; The Modern School[198] in 1896; Dumbarnie Orphanage in 1898; Woodlands School in 1905 (originally established in 1888, but under a different name); Landour Boarding and Day School in 1906; Vincent Hill School and College in 1922 and Hampton Court School in 1922.

Over the years, most of the above-mentioned schools closed down owing to a host of factors that included declining revenues, shortage of staff, and death of founders or lack of financial support from promoters. In this chapter, we discuss the few schools that are still going strong and are today rated amongst the finest schools in the country.

Convent of Jesus and Mary, Waverley

The Waverley Convent School was founded in 1845 and is the oldest school in the Himalayas that is still in operation and bestowing quality education to thousands of students from all over the country. It was established and is managed by the Congregation of Religious of Jesus and Mary—a Roman Catholic group of women who were dedicated to serve the poor and destitute.

It is built on the Waverley Estate, which is believed to have derived its name from a Sir Walter Scott novel titled *Waverley*, and is located at a towering altitude of over 7,000 feet with views of nature that can leave anyone's mouth agape.

The Waverley Estate was bought by Bishop Borghi from an Italian, Paolo Solaroli, a mercenary solider who was loaded with riches. His wealth can probably be attributed to the fact that he was a financial advisor for Begum Sumru of Sardhana (near Meerut in the current state of Uttar Pradesh). It is said that her

---

[198]Not to be confused with Mussoorie Modern School that was established post-independence and was in operation until a few decades ago.

inheritance was valued at a whopping 18 billion Deutsche Mark in 1953. I bet the job for her financial advisor would've been no less in demand than that of a research advisor on Wall Street today.

Waverley Convent School (extreme back) in circa 1866. This school was established in 1845—on the Waverley Estate—and continues to provide quality education for girls. (Picture courtesy: Hotel Savoy, Mussoorie)

Bishop Borghi had also bought land towards the Landour side of town to establish the school, but the Sisters found it unsuitable as it was too far out. And so, eventually, the bishop bought the Waverley Estate, which was a 9-acre property with three houses in existence: Waverley, Belmont and Thistle Bank. Boarding schools came up at Waverley and Belmont, while Thistle Bank was and still is the Chaplain's residence.[199]

Five nuns, with Mother Gonzaga as the superior, arrived in bullock carts from Dehradun[200] to establish this institution,

---

[199]'History of the School', *Convent of Jesus and Mary, Waverley*, www.cjmwaverley. org/School-history.aspx
[200]Ibid.

which is today regarded as one of the finest school for girls in the entire region.

'The Convent School on the Waverley Hill has been long and favourably known as a first class educational institution for girls...'[201]

An early twentieth century postcard showing the campus of Waverley Convent School. This 9-acre estate originally had three buildings; Waverley, Belmont and Thistle Bank. The building seen in the backdrop is the Waverley building.

Originally, Waverley was meant for children who could afford to pay the full fees. The boarding school started off with just seven boarders and a handful of day-scholars, and the lessons were—and no, you will never be able to guess them—drawing and music! Seems about right, doesn't it? Learning the scientific formula for water would seem so monotonous when you could create a sketch of a deep-blue river gushing down the high hills or tune into the melody of the rippling waters and create a tune of your own to mingle with the sounds of nature.

---

[201]Bodycot F., *Guide to Mussoorie* (Mussoorie: Mafasilite Printing Works, 1907), 37.

Belmont was a second school that took in orphans and had admissions at lower rates for underprivileged children; it was later amalgamated into Waverley and is today a junior school.[202]

Waverley offers education from Class I to XII and has close to 350 boarders and 250 day-scholars.

St. George's College

The Capuchin friars[203] of Italy founded St. George's College in 1853. But wait! Before moving further, let's travel back in time to the late seventeenth century. Marco d'Aviano, a Capuchin friar, helped the Roman Emperor in defeating the Ottoman Turks in the battle of Vienna (1683). How this victory changed the balance of power in Europe is another story but let's focus on the numerous bags of coffee captured from the vanquished Turks.

Legend has it that the Roman soldiers found this coffee too bitter to drink. The friar recommended sweetening the coffee by adding a bit of milk. The resultant light-brown coloured drink brought much joy to the soldiers who decided to name it in honour of the blessed Marco d'Aviano.

Selecting the name was a cinch! The light brown colour of the new drink matched the friar's habit and, hence, the name 'Cappuccino'—after the 'Capuchin' friars.[204]

Catapulting now to the mid-nineteenth century and to St. George's College, established for providing quality education to

---

[202]'History of the School', *Convent of Jesus and Mary, Waverley*, www.cjmwaverley.org/School-history.aspx

[203]The Order of Friars Minor Capuchin (OFM Cap.) is a religious order of Franciscan Friars within the Catholic Church. The Order was founded around 1525 and is headquartered in Rome, Italy. 'The History of the Capuchins', *Ordo Fratrum Minorum Capuccincrum*, 14 July 2020, https://www.ofmcap.org/en/cappuccini/the-history-of-the-capuchins

[204]Ibid.

British Catholic children—the school was started at 'Manor House', a vast 400-acre estate in Barlowganj that was purchased from Mr Hutton. In 1866, St. Fidelis School was started in the same campus with twenty-nine children transferred from the Catholic Orphan Asylum at Shimla. Father Macken was the first principal of both schools.[205] Father James Doogan was the principal from 1873 to 1894.

In 1894, the 'brown robed' Capuchins handed over the reins of both schools to the 'white robed' Patrician brothers from Ireland, and they have been managing the school ever since.

An early 1900s view of St. George's College. The area on top of the crest was cleared to pave the way for a large ground that is known as the 'top flat'. (Picture courtesy: St. George's College, Mussoorie)

Brother Haverty had the hill levelled in the early 1900s to pave the way for the famous 'Top Flat' or the large ground at the top of the crest.[206] Brother Phelan got the old building of Manor House reconstructed on the Top Flat in a Gothic design, with classical arches and columns in 1936. The woods surrounding the school had plenty of wild animals, particularly leopards, bears and foxes.

---

[205]St. George's College and St. Fidelis School were merged in 1948.

[206]'Years Old Legacy', *St. George's College*, www.sgconline.ac.in/years-old-legacy

The southern-spur of the estate is even named 'Fox-hill', owing to the abundance of foxes. A clock, especially procured from famous J. B. Joyce and Co,[207] London, was installed atop the building on Top Flat.[208] This clock, that chimed every fifteen minutes, also kept away wild animals from the surrounding woods. Ingenious move indeed!

The Whytebank Castle in the 1980s. It was built in the nineteenth century as the residence of General Barlow after whom Barlowganj locality is named. Maharaja Duleep Singh, son of Maharaja Ranjeet Singh and the last ruler of Sikh Empire, stayed in this building during 185–1854 when he was deposed by the British and send to Mussoorie. (Picture courtesy: St. George's College, Mussoorie)

Its rising popularity made it a gurukul for young princes from various royal houses of India. The old Whytebank Castle, on the adjoining knoll, once a grand residence of General Barlow, was

---

[207]J. B. Joyce & Co is a clock manufacturing company founded in Shropshire in England. Established in 1690, this company is regarded amongst the oldest clock manufacturers in the world.

[208]'Years Old Legacy', *St. George's College*, www.sgconline.ac.in/years-old-legacy

taken over to house the young princes. These parlour boarders enjoyed separate rooms, a private mess and personal security guards. A suspension bridge connected the two ridges to enable easy passage between the school and the 'royal quarters'.

Mr Hugh Gantzer, who studied at St. George's in the 1940s— and had a prince from the royal family of Jind as a classmate— once told me that despite enjoying the comforts and luxury of the castle, these scions of royal families felt lonely and wanted to stay with other students in the dormitories.

Maharaja Duleep Singh, son of Maharaja Ranjeet Singh, the last ruler of Sikh Empire, was deposed by the British and send to Mussoorie in the mid-nineteenth century after the British annexed the kingdom of Punjab. Did the young maharaja stay at the Whytebank Castle?

Ask any alumnus of St. George's and you will get an affirmative nod and a loud 'Yes!'

'He was staying in this castle; he is part of our school history,' vehemently argues Rajeev, one of my batchmates.

But just a few years ago, a researcher of Indian origin arrived in Mussoorie from the United Kingdom, claiming to be an 'expert' on the life history of Maharaja Duleep Singh. And as all the teachers, students and alumni members expectantly sat in the auditorium—eagerly awaiting his affirmation that Duleep Singh stayed at the erstwhile castle and played cricket in the school premises—the researcher dropped a bombshell.

'Duleep Singh stayed at Castle Hill Estate in Landour; he had no connection with your school,' the gentleman announced. 'Believe me, I have done several years of research on the young king,' he added. Everyone was utterly disappointed, yet we had no option but to keep quiet.

But a few years later, while I was going through old manuscripts and journals, I came across a letter written by Dr John Login (under whose care the maharaja was placed at Mussoorie) to Lord Dalhousie dated 10 May 1852: 'As His Highness's residence is at some distance from Mussoorie [...] I have been able to clear a sufficient level space for a playground on the Manor House[209] Estate, so as to admit of his playing cricket, in which he takes great delight.'[210]

This proves, and beyond doubt, that the maharaja stayed at Barlowganj at The Whytebank Castle built by General Barlow—and that he played cricket at the grounds of St. George's College!

For some unknown reason, The Whytebank Castle was sold by St. George's around 1990, and the heritage building was brought down to be replaced by a five-star hotel.

On the subject of history, one must not forget the seven Olympic hockey champions nurtured at St. George's College (see chapter 16.) The four houses in St. George's are named after its four hockey champions: Tapsell's (blue house), Cullen's (green house), Marthins' (yellow house) and Gateley's (red house).

In 1939, the school acquired the Whymper's Pool, adjoining the ruins of the Crown Brewery. This pool that was once used for supplying water to the brewery was later used as a swimming pool for students. Locals firmly believe that this pool and the adjoining area are haunted.

I'm not spooking you, readers. It's a fact that over the years, several people have mysteriously drowned in this pool. Mr Gopal Bhardwaj recounts two deaths in the 1960s—a boy who studied in Rama Devi School and another boy who belonged to a family who owned a famous photo studio in Mussoorie. I too remember a couple of deaths in the 1990s.

'A mysterious force pulls people down into the pool,' one senior citizen once told me.

---

[209]As mentioned earlier, The Manor House estate is the original name of the estate where St. George's College was founded. This estate is nearly 5 kilometres away from The Castle Hill Estate.

[210]Excerpts from a letter written by Dr. Login to the then Governor General Lord Dalhousie dated 10 May 1852. Lady Login L.C., *Sir John Login and Duleep Singh* (London: W.H. Allen & Co, 1890), 289.

Thankfully, no untoward incident happened to any St. George's boy, and the use of the pool was permanently discontinued in 1994, when a state-of-the art pool was constructed within the school campus.

Miss Universe Sushmita Sen inaugurated the auditorium and library building in 1994, but the senior boys were visibly disappointed with the function. 'She should have been called to inaugurate the swimming pool instead. Maybe she might have even taken a dip in the pool,' quipped one of the senior boys many years later.

Well, boys will be boys.

The who's who of the country have studied here, and the list is long. Travel writer Mr Hugh Gantzer, Lieutenant General Anil Kumar Bhatt,[211] Bollywood actors Saeed Jaffery and Kanwaljeet Singh, singer Lucky Ali and the list goes on.

Woodstock School

In the early 1850s, few British officers and American missionaries decided to establish a school for girls at Mussoorie. A company was formed for this purpose and, subsequently in 1854, the Protestant Girls' School opened at Cainville House in Landour.

Help was sought from the London Society for Promotion of Female Education in the East, who promptly sent four ladies to take up the charge of the school. After arriving in Calcutta[212] one of the ladies—who apparently was struck by Cupid during the long voyage—decided to get married and never reached Mussoorie. The other three ladies, Mrs Bignell, Miss Artoun and Miss Birch, established the school at Cainville House.[213]

---

[211]Former Military Secretary and also Director General Military Operations

[212]Present-day Kolkata

[213]'Over 160 Years of Proud History in India', *Woodstock School*, https://www.woodstockschool.in/about/history

A few years later, Woodstock House was purchased from Colonel Reilly, and the school was relocated there (later, adjoining Upper Woodstock and Woodstock Cottage were incorporated into the school) and, in 1862, the Protestant Girls' School was rechristened as Woodstock School.[214]

Old timers still refer to Woodstock as the 'Company' school. I do not have any clear answers as to why the school got this name. Was it because British army officers founded it and hence people connected the school with The East India Company? Or was it that a company was formed to float the school?

Anyway, let's move further to 1871 when lack of funds led to the closure of this institution and the property was put up for sale. Two Presbyterian missionaries—they do deserve a special mention—Reverend Woodside and Dr Samuel Kellogg (after whom the Kellogg's Church at Landour was named) urged a woman from the Presbyterian Church in USA to purchase it and run the school for the children of American missionaries. US $10,000 was raised for the purchase of the school[215] and Woodstock reopened in 1874.

Woodstock was primarily a girls' school, but boys up to twelve years of age were also admitted. It followed the American pattern of education and was primarily meant to cater to missionary children. However, children from non-missionary families also enrolled in large numbers. Separate hostels in 1926 opened the gates for older boys.

In April 1910—during the time when the Halley's Comet was expected to make its periodic appearance—as the students gathered for their evening prayers, a sudden storm tore off the roof of the building; windows started rattling, and all candles were extinguished while the dark room was filled with dust and debris. One girl started screaming with terror. 'The comet's tail's

---

[214]Ibid.
[215]Ibid.

come! The comet's tail's come!' and the mortified girls clung to each other in fear. Meanwhile, amidst the mayhem, the principal calmly continued his prayer.[216]

In 1942, following the Japanese invasion, refugees from Burma, Malaysia and Thailand started pouring in. Woodstock took in a large number of children. Perhaps it was from then onwards that Woodstock has been immensely popular with international students.

In 1954, it became the first school in Asia to gain US accreditation, and the rest is history. Today, Woodstock is amongst the premier schools of the country and attracts a large number of international students.

Wynberg Allen School

The Wynberg Allen School has risen from very humble and benevolent origins. Its roots go back to 1887 when a group of friends, Alfred Powell, Dr J.H. Condon, and Arthur Foy and his wife met at Kanpur and decided to set up a school at Mussoorie[217] for orphans and destitute children of European or Anglo-Indian descent. It started off in 1888 as the Christian Training School and Orphanage with two pupils—orphans by the name of Peter and Mary Cables—under the charge of Mrs Eugenia West.

The first classes began at the Rockville bungalow, which is often referred to as the 'haunted house' (its history would be fascinating, no doubt) at Jabarkhet, along the road to Tehri Garhwal. Nothing great can be said about either the school's early infrastructure or its location. It was a decrepit and uninspiring building located in an area frequented by wild animals and often visited by intense lightning and unforgiving monsoon rains. To

[216]Ibid.

[217]'History', *Wynberg Allen School*, www.wynbergallen.com/cms/details.php?pgID=sb_1

add to the woes of the early inhabitants: water had to be fetched in buckets from a nearby stream, supplies through mules from Landour and kerosene lamps for light and firewood to beat the bitter cold. No wonder the purpose of the place was philanthropic because no degree of monetary allure could motivate someone to push themselves through such hardships. If the school had funds and space, no child was sent back—even if the parents couldn't afford to pay the fee. And Mrs West put her heart and soul to care for the pupils until her untimely demise in 1895.

Around 1893, a fire is said to have damaged much of the school building when a bhatta[218] under the building is reported to have burst,[219] although the students and teachers luckily escaped unhurt. This accident forced the school to shift from Rockville to two bungalows in the Castle Hill Estate, albeit temporarily.

The patrons scouted for permanent and proper premises; their efforts came to fruition in 1894 when the school was moved to the Wynberg

Wynberg Schools, Mussoorie

WYNBERG GIRLS' HIGH SCHOOL,

HENRY ALLEN MEMORIAL BOYS' HIGH SCHOOL

Inter-Denominational Protestant Schools with Exceptionally Brilliant Educational Record.

Situated in the Healthiest Part of Mussoorie. Staffed with Graduates from British, American and Indian Universities.

Children taken special care of by well-trained Matrons and Nurses.

Fees Fixed in Accordance with the Income of European and Anglo-Indian Parents.

Apply :—
H.W.M. SADLEIR, B.A. (Cantab)

An advertisement of Wynberg Allen School published in a 1936 guidebook. (Source: The Rambler, A Mussoorie Miscellany, Mussoorie: Mafasilite Press)

---

[218]Brick kiln

[219]Bond R., *The Story of Wynberg Allen Mussoorie* (Mussoorie: Art Printing Press, 1988), 1.

Estate,[220] where the junior school is currently located. This estate once housed the Masuri Hotel, managed by Bobby Hesseltine, before it was closed down to make way for Wynberg Allen School in 1894. But the shift to Wynberg Estate was made possible only through generous donations.

H.G. Meakin donated a sum of ₹20,000. He was a brewer and the founder of what today has become Mohan Meakin Ltd., the maker of Indian brands such as Old Monk rum, Golden Eagle and Lion beers. But he went beyond the sum that he directly contributed. It is said that he gave explicit instructions to the architect to debit to him the cost of construction and of improving the various buildings in the school campus. Such determination to ensure the revival and welfare of the school arose from a tragic event in his life—his son had died when he was just six-years-old, and Meakin wanted to buy the school in his memory.

Once the move to the Wynberg Estate was made, the school started to flourish with the number of students increasing rapidly. In 1905, the school adopted 'Excelsior' (Latin for 'higher') as its motto, inspired by the 1842 poem of the same name by H.W. Longfellow.

Few years after shifting to the Wynberg Estate, the name of the school also changed distinctly to 'Wynberg Homes for the Poor European and Anglo-Indian Children' or simply, 'Wynberg Homes'.

After Mussoorie got its first electric lights, the children were taken for a 'treat' to watch a movie at the Electric Picture Palace cinema hall—perhaps most of the children watched a motion picture for the first time.[221]

H.D. Allen, a Kanpur based businessman and a philanthropist,

---

[220]'History', *Wynberg Allen School*, www.wynbergallen.com/cms/details.php?pgID=sb_1
[221]Bond R., *The Story of Wynberg Allen Mussoorie* (Mussoorie: Art Printing Press, 1988), 11.

took over as the chairman of Wynberg Homes society in 1918. Allen proposed a separate school for senior boys, as until that time, boys older than twelve could not study at the school.[222] Although Allen passed away a year later, his dreams were realized soon thereafter. With generous contributions from his family, the school was able to purchase the nearby 'Bala Hissar' Estate— former home to Dost Mohammed, an exiled Amir of Afghanistan. The new school for boys, called the Henry Allen Memorial Boys School, opened in 1920.

Interestingly the 'old building' at Bala Hissar—that was once the residence of the Amir—was regarded as 'jinxed' as per reports in *A Mussoorie Miscellany*.[223] Several years before the place was taken over by the school, Captain Charles Henry Deane Spread of the Invalid Establishment at Landour was killed at Bala Hissar after he was struck by lightning. The unfortunate captain was developing some photographic plates. It was when he was collecting rainwater from a drainpipe during a heavy shower when he was struck dead.[224] Another lightning strike at Bala Hissar sent a certain Mr Fitzpatrick to his maker.

Around 1925, lighting struck one of the buildings at Bala Hissar (not the identical one where Captain Spread was killed[225]) one final time, but this time Mr Mackintosh, the principal of the boys' school, was saved by providence. It so happened that Mackintosh, much against his will, went to the cinema and when he returned to school during an intense thunderstorm, he found that his room was on fire—ostensibly struck by lightning.[226]

But nothing to worry about now; nearly a century has passed and no lighting strike has been reported since.

---

[222]Ibid.

[223]The Rambler, *A Mussoorie Miscellany* (Mussoorie: Mafasilite Press, 1936), 74.

[224]Ibid.

[225]Ibid.

[226]Ibid, 75.

During World War II, several ex-students joined the armed forces and a special mention needs to be made of Pilot Officer Charles Dyson who received the 'Distinguished Flying Cross'. Dyson was engaged in an intense dogfight with Italian fighter planes. Showing extraordinary courage and flying skills, Dyson shot down six Italian aircrafts in just fifteen minutes.[227]

Other notable alumni included Elizabeth Davenport, who as a fifteen-year-old broke the all-India record in javelin throw in 1953; Ian Loughran who broke the world gliding record at a competition in Poland; Major Harsh Bahuguna, a mountaineer who scaled Mount Everest in 1965; Roy Andrew Massey, who served the Indian Air Force and received Vir Chakra in the 1971 war after he shot down three Pakistani Sabre Jets.[228]

The four houses in Wynberg are named after its four benefactors: Allen (blue house), Condon (green house), Foy (yellow house) and Powell (red house).

From 1963, co-education was introduced in the school. Today the school has over 700 students from across the country, some from even beyond the borders, and imparts quality education, keeping true to its tough inception and traditions.

Oak Grove School

The Oak Grove School was established in 1888 by the East India Railway Company.[229] The company purchased the 'Oak Grove Estate' at Jharipani to set up the school and the institution was named after this estate.

The objective of this school was to impart education along the lines of schools in England to the children of railway employees who were working in India and could not afford to send their

---

[227]Bond R., *The Story of Wynberg Allen Mussoorie* (Mussoorie: Art Printing Press, 1988), 21.

[228]Ibid, 36–37.

[229]Kinney T., *The Echo Guide to Mussoorie* (Mussoorie: Echo Press, 1908), 76.

wards to England. Education was highly subsidized (it still is) while scholarships were also granted to deserving boys and girls.

'Nothing is left undone to turn out boys and girls educationally, physically and morally, as nearly equal to those brought up in the United Kingdom as the different conditions would allow.'[230]

The school buildings were designed by R. Roskell Bayne,[231] the then chief architect of East Indian Railway and were built under the supervision of W. Drysdale, the company's engineer. In 2009, these buildings, along with three others, made it to India's list of nominees for UNESCO World Heritage Status for 2011.

Oak Grove has separate schools for senior boys and senior girls in the same campus, along with a junior school.

During its formative years, Oak Grove faced water shortages as there were no springs on the estate, but the right to obtain water from Mossy Falls was obtained and pipelines were laid, which resolved the water woes.

Lieutenant Colonel A.C. Chapman (1888–1912) was the first headmaster of Oak Grove who served this institution for nearly twenty-four years.

Adjacent to Oak Grove at Fairlawn Estate, another railway school was in operation since 1877, run by the Scinde, Punjab and Delhi Railway Company (SP&DR) as an off-shoot of the Lahore Railway School. It was a co-educational institute for wards of SP&DR employees, but boys were admitted at the age of twelve. In 1886, it was renamed North Western Railway School after SP&DR was merged with the North Western State Railway. In 1894, as this school battled issues like shortage of staff and accommodation, it was merged with Oak Grove School. Fairlawn Estate was later purchased by Deb Shumsher Jung Bahadur Rana, the exiled Prime Minister of Nepal, and this property became popularly known as Nepal House.

---

[230]Ibid, 77.

[231]The Rambler, *A Mussoorie Miscellany* (Mussoorie: Mafasilite Press, 1936), 62.

Oak Grove had a swimming pool (60 feet by 20 feet), which was fed by natural springs.[232] Children were encouraged to participate in sports such as cricket, hockey, football, tennis and badminton. No wonder Oak Grove produced several Olympic hockey gold medallists for India (see chapter 16).

The first grave in Mussoorie, that of Sir Charles Farrington, is located within the Oak Grove campus (see chapter 7).

Today Oak Grove is home to more than 600 children from across the country, and has a reputation of being the best government-run boarding school in the country.

Hampton Court School

Convent of Jesus and Mary, Hampton Court, was established in 1922, the second school to be opened in the town by the Congregation of Religious of Jesus and Mary.

These Roman Catholic Sisters were already running the Waverley Convent School in Mussoorie for girls, and Hampton Court was started as a preparatory school for young boys—although later Hampton Court was turned into a co-educational school.

A deep-dive into history and we find that the Hampton Court Estate was named after sixteenth century Hampton Court Palace in Surrey near London. This estate housed the Hampton Court hotel until the mid-1890s. Hampton Court Hotel was regarded as amongst the few good hotels in the town as observed in an 1890 guidebook, 'Hampton Court Hotel is quiet and comfortable,'[233] although in a later guidebook, as mentioned in *A Mussoorie Miscellany*,[234] this hotel is also referred to as the 'Calcutta Hotel.'

---

[232]Kinney T., *The Echo Guide to Mussoorie* (Mussoorie: Echo Press, 1908), 78.

[233]Hawthorne R., *The Beacon's Guide to Mussoorie* (Mussoorie: The Beacon Press, 1890).

[234]The Rambler, *A Mussoorie Miscellany* (Mussoorie: Mafasilite Press, 1936), 61.

In 1876–1877, Hampton Court School was started on these premises by Reverend Henry Sells.[235] In 1895, this school was taken over by Miss Florence Holland and converted into a preparatory school. It came to be known as 'Miss Holland's School.' Under the wings of Miss Holland, who was an educationist of repute, the school developed a reputation for high educational standards. The advertisements by the school also spoke about, 'fine grounds, large and airy buildings' and even 'home cows'.[236]

'[…] there is no branch of education in which the pupils of Hampton Court have not scored constant and enviable success,'[237] observed a 1907 guidebook.

By 1921, an aging Miss Holland sought retirement, and Hampton Court was put up for sale and purchased by the Roman Catholic sisters who started Hampton Court Preparatory Boy's School in 1922 from Classes I to IV (although later it was made a co-educational institution).

The formative years were difficult due to lack of teachers. For several years, nuns from New Delhi Day School were asked to come to Hampton Court during the summer months. The building also underwent major renovations in 1933. The rest is history.

Over the years, Hampton Court gained the reputation of being one of the finest preparatory schools in north India. Old timers recall that students from Hampton Court were granted admission into St. George's College or Waverley Convent without any entrance exam.

'I often bump into "Hampty boys",' remarked my senior Randeep Grewal recently. 'Last month, I met an MLA from Punjab. Somehow, I casually remarked about going to Mussoorie and to my utter surprise the gentleman turned out to be a "Hampty" boy, just a few years senior to me!' Randeep exclaimed over the phone.

---

[235]Ibid.

[236]Bodycot F., *Guide to Mussoorie* (Mussoorie: Mafasilite Printing Works, 1907), 36.

[237]Kinney T., *The Echo Guide to Mussoorie* (Mussoorie: Echo Press, 1908), 82.

Several movies have also been filmed in the school campus, most notable being the Rajesh Khanna starrer *Karm* (1977).

Some Schools for Indians

Prior to Independence, most of the English medium schools catered to the European and Anglo-Indian children, although some scions of Indian royalty also found admission in these schools.

For the local Indian population, the first vernacular medium school was Islamia School, started in one room at Landour by Maulvi Mohammad Sayid in 1906.[238] Arya Kanya Pathshala was the first school for girls opened in 1917, followed by Sanatan Dharm Kanya Pathshala (another girls' school) in 1928—both these schools are still going strong. Ghananand High School[239] at Kincraig was started in 1927 by Radha Ballabh Khanduri[240] in the memory of his brother.

Some English medium schools, too, came up after 1947. These include Mussoorie Public School, floated by a group of local residents, and Mussoorie International School.

Do you have a cigarette?

Walking alone at night on the road near Sikandar Hall, old Crown Brewery or Whymper's pool? Better keep a pack of cigarettes in your pocket and, for good measure, keep a box of matches too!

But why?

Legend has it that on dark and desolate nights, when a dense

---

[238]Hari Har Lal P., *The Doon Valley Down the Ages* (New Delhi: Interprint, 1993), 189.

[239]It is now Ghananand Rajkiye Inter College and provides schooling up to Class XII.

[240]He was the grandfather of Major General B.C. Khanduri, former Chief Minister of Uttarakhand.

blanket of fog engulfs the road, a ghost often accosts the lonely pedestrians.

Now you must be wondering, why the cigarettes and the matchbox? Let me narrate the ghastly experience of Mr Sharma who chanced to venture alone on the Barlowganj Road late at night, many, many years ago.

'A friend who lived near Kincraig invited me for dinner and it was around 1 a.m. when I left his house,' Mr Sharma narrated. 'There were hardly any motorbikes or cars in those times. I ambled along to my house in Barlowganj in the chilly dark night, armed with a small flashlight and an umbrella.'

As he reached within 200 metres of Sikandar Hall, someone called to him.

'My dear fellow, do you have a cigarette?' a raspy voice with a Cockney accent asked.

As the startled Mr Sharma looked around to locate the source of the query, he saw the silhouette of a man wearing an overcoat, standing to his right at the edge of the road.

'Do you have a cigarette?' he heard the same raspy voice, sounding a bit irritated this time round.

'Oh, it's an Englishman, maybe he lives nearby at Sikandar Hall, Whitefield Hall or..' thought Mr. Sharma, a bit relieved now.

'I'm sorry, Sir, I don't smoke,' he replied apologetically while trying to peer through the fog to recognize the gentleman.

Before Mr Sharma could realize it, a hand shot out of the shadows and slapped him. He felt a searing pain shoot through his cheek and ears.

'Next time, carry a cigarette,' the man boomed.

Before Mr Sharma could retort, the shadow disappeared.

'Although I could see the profile of his body but, strangely, I could not see the silhouette of his head,' Mr Sharma told me.

He recounted that after this incident he heard from several people who had encountered this seemingly 'headless' ghost.

'He accosted many people from Barlowganj and also the

washermen from Dhobi Ghat. Asking for a cigarette first, and then also for a matchbox,' Mr Sharma said while narrating that after getting both a cigarette and a matchbox, the ghost would disappear.

But nobody could make out the head of this ghost. Perhaps he was a British army officer whose head had been cut off in some gory battle of the past.

But who was he? Why was he seen in this location? How was his head cut off? Why was he asking for a cigarette? These are some questions which, it seems, will remain unanswered till eternity.

A few years ago, a friend of mine gathered some courage to try to 'meet' this headless ghost. So one night, he ventured out alone on this road carrying a box of cigarettes and a matchbox (while two of his friends waited in the car a short distance away, ready to rush to his rescue). He even connected with them on a call and kept the mobile in his pocket as he walked towards Sikandar Hall.

He crossed the old bungalow, then the narrow bridge beyond it, and went past Whymper's pool but, fortunately or unfortunately, the British ghost was not in a mood to borrow a cigarette that night.

Or maybe increasing urbanization and rising traffic have driven the ghost away.

'He is still lurking somewhere, waiting to pounce on some unsuspecting pedestrian. Who knows!' says Mr Gopal Bhardwaj with a twinkle in his eyes.

10

CHEERS FOR THE TIPPLERS!

The 'Indian pale ale' has a tale of its own. And hosting one of the earliest breweries to be set up in the country, Mussoorie figures prominently in this tale.

As the empire sought to gain ground in India, the scorching summers were made more unbearable as the local Indian beer failed to excite the palates of British tipplers. As early as 1716, 'pale ale'[241] and 'Burton ale'[242] were promptly imported from England—after all, it was important to keep the army in good humour. These were soon replaced by 'porter' beer, which had gained rapid popularity across Europe. Porter did not suit the warm climes of India, and the long sea voyages; 'It arrived in India flat, sour and undrinkable.'[243] But it seems the British had little choice.

In the later part of the eighteenth century, George Hodgson, a London brewer, 'had a "eureka!" moment.'[244] Hodgson's 'Bow Brewery' developed the perfect brew for India. It had higher alcohol content while hops[245] were put in beer barrels to preserve it on its long voyage and also to stabilize it against the constant

---

[241]Ale is a variety of beer that is fermented using yeast at warmer temperatures. Ale has a dark colour and a strong, fruity flavour. Pale ale is made with pale malt and has a lighter colour compared to other ales.

[242]Burton ale is a variety of ale that is dark coloured and sweeter compared to the normal ale. This ale is named after the town, Burton-on-Trent, in England.

[243]Brown P., *Hops and Glory: One Man's Search for Beer that Built the British Empire* (London: Pan Macmillan, 2009), 163.

[244]Ibid, 161.

[245]Hops are the flowers or cones of a plant called *Humulus lupulus*. They were added to beer to keep it longer and preserve its aroma and flavour.

rocking motion in the ships.[246]

This improvised beer came to be known as 'Indian pale ale' or IPA; it was widely advertised and became hugely popular.

The Mussoorie Brew

In the eighteenth and nineteenth centuries, brewing could take place only in cool climates 'when wild yeasts lay dormant'.[247] The warm climate of the Indian plains was a deterrent to brewing until the 1830s, when hill stations opened new avenues for the brewers.

India's earliest brewery was established in the Queen of the Hills in 1830, and the pale ale and strong ale produced here in the latter half of the nineteenth century came to be in great demand amongst the tipplers, giving 'Indian pale ale' a run for its money. Mussoorie's beer was much sought after in cantonments such as Agra, Allahabad, Dehradun, Ferozepur, Jabalpur, Jalandhar, Jhansi, Ludhiana, Meerut and Saharanpur. The legendary poet Mirza Ghalib is believed to have travelled often from Delhi to Meerut to procure his quota of the Mussoorie brew.[248]

Henry Bohle, a whisky manufacturer from Meerut, saw an opportunity for brewing in the cool climate of the town. Bohle's Brewery (later known as Old Brewery) was set up towards the west of town, at Lynndale Estate. Equipment was painstakingly sourced from England to Calcutta via ships and transported via boats sailing through the Ganges up to Haridwar. Ox-drawn carts

[246]Pryror A., *Indian Pale Ale: An Icon of Empire* in Jonathan Curry-Machado J. (ed.), *Global Histories, Imperial Commodities, Local Interactions* (New York: Palgrave Macmillan, 2013), 40.

[247]Brown P., *Hops and Glory: One Man's Search for Beer that Built the British Empire* (London: Pan Macmillan, 2009), 57.

[248]Mishra P.R., 'The Mussoorie brew which had Ghalib hooked', *The Times of India*, 3 October 2015, https://timesofindia.indiatimes.com/city/dehradun/the-mussoorie-brew-which-had-ghalib-hooked/articleshow/49210000.cms?frmapp=yes&from=mdr

carried the equipment from Haridwar to the brewery.

Mr Bohle soon brewed up a storm with Colonel Young.[249] Young first charged Bohle with supplying beer to soldiers from the Landour Cantonment (who came to the brewery with forged passes) and later, Bohle was accused of operating a distillery without a license, something Bohle vehemently denied; he maintained that he was getting whisky from his distillery at Meerut.

Troubles with Young, financial reasons or both made Bohle close down 'Old Brewery' and sell the estate to Parsons in 1832. In 1834, Bohle's estate was purchased from Parsons by John Mackinnon, son-in-law of Bohle, to set up Mussoorie's first school, the Masuri Seminary.

Bohle returned in 1834 for a second innings and established 'Bohle's Brewery' towards the north of the Old Brewery. Meanwhile, in 1850, Mackinnon reopened the Old Brewery. His sons, Philip and Walter, further expanded the brewery business.

The famous Golden Eagle brand of beer owes much of its existence to Mussoorie too. Edward Abraham Dyer, father of the infamous General

Imposing ruins of the 'Old Brewery' at Lynndale estate towards Hathipaon. The building was constructed using thin, red burnt-clay bricks called the 'Lakhori bricks'. Old Brewery was the first brewery of Mussoorie— established in 1830 but closed in 1832. It was reopened by Mr Mackinnon in 1850 and flourished thereafter. This estate is now owned by the DLF Group.

---

[249]Captain Frederick Young is regarded as the founding father of the town, and had a mercurial rise. By 1832 he held the combined offices of Superintendent of Doon and Commandant of Landour Cantonment.

Reginald Edward Dyer,[250] visited his brother, John, a practicing barrister based in Mussoorie. John 'suggested to his brother that he start up the brewing of English beer.'[251] Perhaps John's advice was based on the flourishing brewery business at Mussoorie. In 1855, Edward set up his brewery on the ruins of an earlier one[252]—not at Mussoorie, but at Kasauli. It was named the 'Dyer Breweries', which was later to become Mohan Meakin Breweries.

Meanwhile, Crown Brewery was opened near Barlowganj by Messrs Murch and Dyer in 1867. Whether the Dyer named in this partnership was a relative of General Dyer I cannot say with surety. However, this brewery was closed within two years until 1876, when Messrs Whymper and Co. took over and restarted this brewery.

THE
CROWN BREWERY COMPANY,
"LIMITED."
MUSSOORIE.
CONTRACTORS TO GOVERNMENT,

BREWERS OF PALE AND MILD ALES AND XXX STOUT,

Supply the Public, Messes, Canteens, and Merchants, direct from the Brewery, or through their Agents in Landour, Mussoorie, Dehra, Chuckrata, Saharunpore, Jullundhur, Loodiana, Ferozepore, Agra, Morar, Jhansee, Allahabad, &c.

ALE and STOUT, in wood   :. Rs. 1-12 per gall.
Do.   in bottle ...   ,, 5-0 ,, dbz. qts.
Do.   do.   ...   ,, 2-12 ,, ,, pts.

Rs. 3 charged for casks, and same allowed on return in good condition.

. Eight annas per dozen quarts, and six annas per dozen pints, allowed for empty bottles returned to Brewery, or Agents in Mussoorie.

N.B.—Five and nine gallon casks are convenient loads for one and two coolies respectively, and are suitable for camp use.
J. W. WHYMPER,
Manager,

An advertisement of Crown Brewery that appeared in an 1884 guidebook. (Source: Northam J., Guide to Masuri, Landour, Dehradun and The Hills North of Dehra, Calcutta: Thacker, Spink and Co., 1884, 172)

To supply water to this brewery, a nearby spring was tapped to make a pool known as the Whymper's Pool. Years later, the pool came into the ownership of St. George's College and until the mid-1990s, it was used as a swimming pool by the students.

---

[250]General Dyer is referred to as the 'Butcher of Amritsar' and is considered responsible for the Jallianwala Bagh massacre.
[251]Collett N., *The Butcher of Amritsar General Reginald Dyer* (India: Rupa Publications, 2005), 4.
[252]Ibid, 5.

Brewers by appointment to H. E. the Viceroy and Governor-General of India.

MACKINNON AND CO.,
THE OLD BREWERY, MUSSOORIE,
Established 1850.

Pale Ale, Strong Alo (XXXX), and XXX Porter can now be had at the Brewery, or from the undersigned.

The following are selected from numerous testimonials.

HIMALAYA CLUB,
Mussoorie, July, 1877.

GENTLEMEN:—With reference to your letter of the 9th instant, our consumption for the last three years of your Pale Ale has been about 4 to 6 kilderkins per mensem, and I have pleasure in stating that your Ale, both in cask and bottle, has given entire satisfaction.

Yours faithfully,
(Sd.) T. W. FITCH, *Secretary.*

LANDOUR, 23rd *February,* 1877.

GENTLEMEN:—In reply to your letter of yesterday, I have the honor to inform you that the Beer supplied by you to the Depôt under my command has invariably been of most excellent quality, and that the N. C. Officers and men prefer it to any other which has been at any time issued to them.

I therefore hope that you will have no difficulty in obtaining authority to continue the supply.

(Sd.) J. M. CAMPBELL,
Lieut.-Col., R. A., Comdg. at Landour.

Cash Prices of Ale or Porter in Bottle.

Pale Ale or Porter, Quarts ... ... Rs. 5 0
Do. do. Pints ... ... „ 2 12

The above prices include eight annas per dozen for bottles, which will be allowed when bottles are sent or returned.

Ale or Porter in wood, in casks of 4½, 9, 18, and 36 gallons, at Rs. 1-12 per gallon.

FITCH & CO.,
Sole Agents for Mussoorie.

An advertisement of Mackinnon and Co. in an 1884 guidebook. The brewery manufactured pale ale, strong ale and XXX Porter. (Source: Northam J., Guide to Masuri, Landaur, Dehradun and The Hills North of Dehra, Calcutta: Thacker, Spink and Co., 1884, 169)

Owing to a combination of local spring water, climate and perhaps, better fermentation, Mussoorie brew was widely demanded, especially by the army while keeping the brewers in high spirits too!

On 23 February 1877, Lieutenant Colonel Campbell, Commandant of Landour Cantonment wrote to Mackinnon and Co., '[…] I have the honour to inform you that the beer supplied by you to the depot under my command has invariably been of most excellent quality […] I therefore hope that you have no difficulty in obtaining authority to continue the supply.'[253]

In 1903, the two breweries were brewing about half a million gallons of beer: 'Mussoorie exists chiefly as a health resort and the only manufacture is that of beer at two breweries, which employed 131 men in 1903 and made nearly half a million gallons of beer.'[254]

According to anecdotes, the fortunes of Mackinnon and Co. took a tumble in the early 1900s when one of their competitors put a dead fly in a mug of the beer that was served to General Lord Kitchener, commander-in-chief of British forces in India, causing huge outrage. Kitchener promptly ordered that Mackinnon's beer was never to be served for the troops anymore.[255] However, it is believed that modern technologies that paved the way for brewing in the plains led to the downfall of these breweries, which were closed around the second decade of the twentieth century.

Today, the ruins of Crown Brewery have been replaced by new buildings, while the ruins of Old Brewery remain a testimony to the heydays of the Mussoorie brew.

---

[253]Northam J., *Guide to Masuri, Landaur, Dehradun and The Hills North of Dehra* (Calcutta: Thacker, Spink and Co., 1884), 169.

[254]Imperial Gazetteer of India, *United Provinces of Agra and Oudh: Vol. I* (Calcutta: Superintendent of Government Printing, 1908), 267.

[255]Hari Har Lal P., *The Doon Valley Down the Ages* (New Delhi: Interprint, 1993), 187.

Human Oil Extractors

There was a time in Mussoorie when people of Indian origin shuddered to venture out of their houses after dark. A fear of being abducted by unknown people was widespread. These 'abductors'—who were even referred to as supernatural beings—were believed to abduct any citizen (Indian citizens, to be precise) from the streets after dark.

The first time I heard about these mysterious beings was on a chilly winter evening in the 1980s when, while playing hide-and-seek, one of my friends remarked, 'It is getting dark, we must return to our homes otherwise "Teli" will come and catch us.'

All of us laughed. 'Who is a "Teli"?' I asked mockingly.

'My mother told me that in Mussoorie, Telis come and abduct people after dark,' my friend replied earnestly.

After mocking him some more and a hearty laugh, all of us returned to our homes. Within a few days, we all forgot about the Teli till another reference was made nearly a decade later. While I was collecting titbits about the history of my glorious town, an old timer[256] made a passing reference about Indians being abducted for extracting 'human oil' by Telis.

'What? Are you serious?' I questioned, thinking that the old man had actually gone senile.

'I am telling the truth, my dear boy, human oil was extracted in Mussoorie,' the old man calmly replied.

'Is this a joke, uncle? I have never heard such a ridiculous claim; you must be insane,' I blurted and almost immediately regretted my outburst.

'You can do your own research then,' he replied calmly, got up and walked away.

---

[256]It is my practice to mention names of people only after their due permission. Since this gentleman passed away years ago, I am refraining from disclosing his name.

This conversation piqued my interest in the Telis, aka the human oil extractors, and so began my research about these mysterious characters. I firmly believed that these were fictitious characters, invented by a frivolous mind to spread panic amongst the Indian community.

However, my subsequent research revealed that perhaps I was wrong. Telis were not figments of imagination!

A careful perusal of old journals (a few as old as the mid-nineteenth century) and interactions with senior citizens and historians unearthed some strange and horrific events that had transpired in my town in the pre-independence era. I am sharing them with my readers here.

The Telis!

Imagine going out of your home for an errand after dusk and never to return! This was the scenario in pre-independence era as Indians, particularly the porters and other blue-collared people, were frequently abducted in the dark of the night.

In the 1850s and 1860s, a number of porters or coolies started going missing from the town. The word went around town that they were being abducted by the Telis for extraction of human oil. The fear of Telis led to a large-scale exodus of porters from the town. The British tried to deny such occurrences in a bid to woo the porters to stay in the town.

Lady Constance Frederica Gordon Cumming, who visited Mussoorie in the 1870s, observed in her travelogue,[257] 'To a population thus dependent upon the multitude of human workers, any causes that diminishes the supply is a serious matter. Imagine, then, the effect of a story having, some years ago, been circulated among the hill tribes that the Europeans required a vast supply of

---

[257]Cumming C.F.G., *From the Hebrides to the Himalayas: Vol. II.* (London: Sampson Low, Marston, Searle and Rivington, 1876), 280.

"Pahari oil", and intended to take every hill man, woman, or child, whom they could catch, and hang them up by the heels before a big fire in order to extract their oil! This story was universally believed that all the coolies ran away from Massourie *(read Mussoorie)*, and were only persuaded by slow degrees of return; and for months they continued to work tremblingly, still believing in danger.'

While Lady Constance believed that the word going around the town about the Telis was just a 'story', she was perhaps just being a mouthpiece for the British.

Did the Telis actually exist? Were they humans or supernatural beings? Did they actually abduct people and extract human oil? Why was human oil extracted? Many questions such as these, although unanswered, are pondered over at leisure; albeit amongst a small section of citizenry today—the elderly who have heard fables from their fathers and grandfathers about the Telis.

Let's unravel the mystery. Telis were not supernatural beings but actually humans—in all probability of Chinese origin (as per the vague descriptions shared by two residents who have claimed to have actually seen them. I happened to speak with one of them almost twenty-five years ago, a highly reputed medical practitioner whose word can rarely be doubted). They were believed to be operating in Mussoorie since around the 1860s till the time of Independence.

These cryptic abductors lurked furtively in the dark streets of the town, especially in the outskirts, waiting patiently for their unsuspecting victims. Telis are believed to have operated in a group and would carry large sacks, with which they would trap their victims, often making them unconscious for good measure.

According to Mr Gopal Bhardwaj, Naktu Ram, the former watchman at Lynndale Estate where Bohle's Brewery was located, said that the Telis carried their victims to their settlement, which was located close to the breweries. Naktu Ram claimed to have seen the human oil extractors from a distance as they went about their dreadful business.

Although no one knows much exactly about the process of human oil extraction, it is believed that the oil was extracted from the head and, for this purpose, the victims were hung upside down. Some even say that the victims were hung above a fire. Who knows? None of the victims returned to tell the tale!

It is believed that the Telis were operating from both the breweries—Bohle's Brewery and Crown Brewery—perhaps for the simple reason that it was convenient to dispose off the dead bodies in the furnace. Quite gruesome, isn't it?

It is also widely believed that the buildings of the breweries were haunted. Well, now you know the reason why they were haunted!

But why was human oil extracted? 'The oil was used for medicinal purposes, especially for treating wounded British soldiers,' says Mr Bhardwaj.

So these were the horrifying human oil extractors of Mussoorie who tormented the Indian citizenry for nearly a century.

The doctor and the oil extractors

Dr G, a noted physician of the town, had an encounter with the Telis during the mid-1940s. During a personal communication in 1990s, the old doctor narrated his escapade to me, which I am sharing with the readers here.

Dr G had his residence and clinic near Gandhi Chowk. He was a highly regarded physician, consulted by Indians as well as by the British community. The doctor narrated that it was the autumn of 1946 or 1947 when a messenger came requesting him to urgently accompany him as his master was unwell.

'Considering the urgency of the request, I immediately put some essentials in my physician's bag, which was promptly picked up by the messenger and we marched to the patient's house,' Dr G recalled. 'Dusk was falling when we reached the patient's house on Camel's Back Road. The patient was writhing on the bed, holding his stomach,' he narrated.

Dr G said that after attending to the patient, he waited for some time till the patient showed signs of some relief.

'As I left the house, it was dark. I had forgotten my watch in my clinic but it must have been later than 8 p.m.,' he recalls. Dr G said that he felt a bit uneasy due to the various stories going around the town and as people were being advised not to venture outside after dark. 'I was regretting that I did not ask his servant to accompany me as I hurried towards my house on the dark and desolate road,' he said.

A brisk walk of ten minutes brought him close to the point where Camel's Back Road joined with the Mall Road.

'I was relieved. The Mall Road is well-lit and police guards would be on patrol,' the doctor said. He recalled that, suddenly, he saw two dark shadows emerging from the bushes by the roadside.

'I got the fright of my life as the two shadows approached me. I still vividly recall them to be of small height, wearing something like a cloak or a loose robe. They had small round faces, although I could not see their faces clearly,' Dr G said with a nervous smile on his face as he recalled those anxious moments. He added that before he could gather enough wits to turn back and run, the duo had pounced upon him.

'They pinned me to the ground while trying to cover my mouth with a cloth. "I'm a doctor! I'm a doctor!" I somehow managed to shout,' the doctor said. After hearing that he was a doctor, the duo examined his bag and finding it to contain medicines and other equipment, they left him and disappeared in the darkness.

'This was the most horrifying moment of my life. Henceforth I slept with a gun by my bedside for several months,' he told me, a wry smile on his face.

Ice Wells that Melt Away!

It all started over a pint of beer on a warm summer afternoon. 'For beer lovers, chilled beer is perhaps the quintessential joy, nothing beats it,' remarked my friend Sam Pal, another beer lover.

'It is,' I responded, a bit absent-mindedly. 'Now answer this. How was beer chilled in the absence of electricity and refrigerators?' I was thinking about the Brits and their breweries in Mussoorie.

'Well, I wouldn't believe our fathers and grandfathers drank much beer. They were way more Indian than we are.' He let out a hearty chuckle.

'I mean, how did the British cool their beer? Did they have lukewarm beer? Yuck!'

So here I was, having stumbled upon a fascinating mystery whose answer would quell some of my thirst for an honest history of my hometown. My only earnest hope was to not end up discovering that the Brits liked their beer lukewarm. What a dampener that would be.

And the truth soon came out when I happened to learn about the ice wells—indigenous and natural refrigerators used to cool beer, wine and even preserve meat.

The earliest references to 'ice wells' (later modified to 'ice house') are found in 1780 BC in the ancient city-state of Mari in Syria, and later references are found in the seventh and eighth century BC in China. In Britain, references to ice wells are found in the late seventeenth century.

Making of an ice well

Generally speaking, an ice well resembled a conventional well filled with ice instead of water. But indeed, some structural aspects made it different from a well. One was that its walls were quite thick and lined with bricks; its location was critical too—ice wells that I have come across in Mussoorie are built at locations that, due to the hilly topography, practically get no direct sunlight; lastly, ice wells had a drainage system comprising a drain hole at the bottom, allowing the melted ice to trickle out of the well.

During the winters, after a good snowfall, numerous servants were deployed to collect snow from the surroundings and fill it the ice wells with it.

The well was generally filled in layers—a layer of snow that was beaten to make it dense, then another and then another, till the well was filled to the brim. They were insulated with layers of grass and salt. During the summer, the ice was extracted and used. Generally, it was not used for food as it was considered unhygienic. But it was used for cooling beer and wine.

However, I am told that hotels used to immerse beer and wine in the ice wells (a layer of bottles under a layer of ice), which were then extracted during the summers, chilled to the core. Meat, too, was stored in the wells to preserve it.

Where to find them in Mussoorie?

There were a large number of ice wells in the town. According to estimates by old timers there, were more than twenty ice wells in Mussoorie. All the major hotels had at least one, if not more; the cantonment had several, while a handful of rich and influential gentlemen had personal ice wells dug up in their estates.

In the present, all ice wells seem to have melted away. Actually, the advent of refrigerators made them redundant. Some wells were broken down to accommodate new buildings; some filled with muck and waste over the years.

I have been able to find only two ice wells that are in existence—barely surviving. One is located close to Himalaya Club in Landour that, according to various accounts, was constructed in 1841. Another one is in what was earlier Duggal Villa, located close to Gandhi Chowk.

Both are, of course, not in use, but one can gaze down at them and reconnect to the lost era. Beer lovers can derive solace from the fact that Brits, too, loved chilled beer.

11

HOME AWAY FROM HOME

'Stand still for ten minutes and they will build a hotel on top of you,' observed the master storyteller Ruskin Bond.[258] How true those words are! Instead of mushrooms—hotels, guest houses and home-stays have sprung up on the hill slopes of our town. How many? Maybe 300 or 500? No one knows.

While strolling on the Mall, I am often rudely accosted by motorists.

'Are you a local?' they shout.

'Yes.'

'Where is —— hotel?' is the second question.

Damn, I have never heard this name before, I think.

'I am sorry, boss. I have no idea where it is located,' I sheepishly reply, my ignorance earning me a disdainful look from the questioner. And believe me, this has happened so many times. It seems that almost every day a new hotel or guest house pops up in the town. Tourism officials claim that over a million tourists visit the town annually; no wonder everyone wants a bite of the cherry.

But let's leave *these* modern hotels alone for the moment and rewind the clock to the heydays of Mussoorie. The glorious yesteryears, when hotels were not cluttered, claustrophobic structures, and when hospitality was much more than providing bed and breakfast.

The hotel industry took roots in the Queen of the Hills when

---

[258]Bond R. & Saili S., *Mussoorie and Landour: Days of Wine & Roses* (New Delhi: Roli Books, 2010), 15.

Mr Webb opened a 'hotel for families'.[259] Travel writer Fanny Parks, who stayed in Mussoorie in 1838 and visited this hotel, writes, 'It is an excellent one, and very commodious. There is a ball room, and five billiard tables with slate beds; these slate beds have only just arrived in India, and have very lately been introduced in England.'[260]

Parks did not divulge the name of this hotel nor its location, but I have a strong hunch that this hotel was the Waverley Hotel on the road from the library towards present-day Waverley Convent and was owned by Kreiser, a German gentleman. It was rechristened as Alexandra Hotel in the late nineteenth century.

Himalaya Hotel was located prominently on the Mall Road—at

A view of the Himalaya Hotel (circa 1870). This hotel was replaced by the Himalaya Bank in 1874, Bank of Upper India in 1904 and subsequently Imperial Bank (later State Bank of India) in the twentieth century. This grand building now houses the office of Life Insurance Corporation of India. My great-grandfather established his office in the building seen next to the hotel (circa 1910). (Photographer: T.A. Rust)

[259]Parks F., *Wanderings of a Pilgrim in Search of the Picturesque: Vol. II* (London: Pelham Richardson, 1850), 230.
[260]Ibid.

the site of the present-day State Bank of India—which was replaced by the Himalaya Bank in 1874. 'The Himalayan [sic] Hotel there is the best hotel I have met with in India; and there are also a clubhouse and a good subscription reading room and a library,' wrote Andrew Wilson,[261] a chronicler who stayed here in the early 1870s.

Other early birds included the Masuri[262] Hotel (later changed to Mussoorie), managed by Bobby Hesseltine before it was closed down to make way for Wynberg Allen school in 1894. An 1894 journal[263] refers to this hotel as 'an old established hostelry' that was quite popular with visitors. Hampton Court Hotel (later Calcutta Hotel) had to make way for Hampton Court School in 1876. Another hotel was Woodville Hotel located in Landour. Cecil Hotel opened in 1907 on top of a hillock, barely 100 metres from the library building. The hotel had twenty large rooms and offered a splendid view. It is still operational under the name of Hotel Prince.

But amongst this long list of hotels there is no doubt that Savoy, Charleville and Hakman's made the top bracket.

MUSSOORIE HOTEL,
MUSSOORIE,
ESTABLISHED 1859,
NEAR

The Himalaya Club, Municipal Hall, Post and Telegraph Offices, Castle Hill Lawn Tennis Grounds, Tivoli Gardens, and convenient to the Church and Library.

The locality in which this Hotel is situated has always been remarkably healthy. The premises being extensive and open, are pronounced, on high medical authority, to be in the most salubrious part of this Sanitarium.

Lawn Tennis—Badminton—Billiards.

Every information and assistance rendered to gentlemen proceeding into the interior.

☞ No Extras. ☜

Terms on application to
CLIFFORD WILLARD,
Manager.

An 1884 advertisement of Mussoorie Hotel. (Source: Northam J., Guide to Masuri, Landaur, Dehradun and The Hills North of Dehra, Calcutta: Thacker, Spink and Co., 1884, 179)

[261]Wilson A., *Abode of Snow* (London: William Blackwood and Sons, 1875), 38.
[262]It was known by locals as '*Bobby saheb ka hotel*'.
[263]Northam J., *Guide to Masuri, Landaur, Dehradun and The Hills North of Dehra* (Calcutta: Thacker, Spink and Co., 1884), 60.

Charleville Hotel

'What's in a name?' were the famous lines by the great writer and dramatist William Shakespeare. Two and half centuries later, Hobson (co-promoter and manager of Mussoorie Bank) echoed similar sentiments, and without 'much ado', named his new hotel after his sons, 'Charlie' and 'Billy'. So one of the finest hotels of its era came to be known as 'Charlie–Billy' until the property changed hands and the name was changed to 'Charleville'.

Hotel Charleville was considered to be the finest hotel in Mussoorie. The then Princess of Wales (later crowned Queen Mary) stayed at Charleville during her maiden visit to Mussoorie. In 1959, the hotel premises were taken over by the government to establish the Lal Bahadur Shastri National Academy of Administration (LBSNAA).

The original building of the hotel premises came up in 1842,[264] although in 1854, General Wilkinson (the then owner) is also believed to have added some buildings. In 1857, a girls' school was started (perhaps it was a part of Waverley Convent School) on these premises but it was not until 1877 that the hotel business

---

[264]Kinney T., *The Echo Guide to Mussoorie* (Mussoorie: Echo Press, 1908), 91.

started on these premises, after Hobson, a banker, purchased the estate from the General. After Hobson passed away in 1880, the Mussoorie Bank acquired the hotel—perhaps our banker was unable to pay his debt.

The property was leased to Messrs T. Fitch and C. Stowell and was managed by Mr Treherne. Then came Mr Henry Wultzer, a German 'of a stock of hotel keepers[265]'—who took over Charleville from Fitch and Stowell in 1884.

In 1887, Wultzer outrightly purchased the hotel from the bank and expanded the premises. It soon had 112 rooms as well as spacious drawing rooms, a dining room, a ball room, card rooms, a billiard room and two tennis courts; Charleville was regarded as the largest hotel outside Bombay.[266] The hotel also offered a captivating view of the snow-clad Himalayan peaks.

The grandeur of Charleville prompted the then Princess of Wales (who was later crowned Queen Mary) to stay at Charleville during her maiden visit to Mussoorie. 'This being the only hotel in India where Her Royal Highness honoured by staying at during her Indian tour in 1906,' Kinney[267] observes.

The renowned author and poet Rudyard Kipling stayed at Charleville in 1888 on his only visit to Mussoorie, but perhaps he could not bear the incessant July rains of Mussoorie and had to make a hasty exit, never to return again. The hotel had its own orchard and kitchen garden and even housed a poultry farm, piggery and dairy. A post and telegraph office, too, was located within the premises. The unique seal at this post office bore the word 'Charleville'. To my knowledge, only two hotels, and both in Mussoorie, were privileged to have post office seals in their name: Charleville and Savoy.

The prospering hotel business prompted Wultzer to form a

---

[265]Ibid, 92.

[266]Ibid, 90.

[267]Ibid.

CHARLEVILLE HOTEL,

Happy Valley, MUSSOORIE.

Proprietors : Wutzler, Limited,

CATERERS,

BY ROYAL WARRANT TO

T. R. H. The Prince and Princess of Wales

BY APPOINTMENT TO

H. R. H. The Duke of Connaught,

Their Excellencies Earl of Minto, Lord Curzon of Kedleston, the Earl of Elgin and the Marquis of Lansdowne, late Viceroys and Governors-General of India, the late H. R. H. the Duke of Clarence ; H. I. H. the Czar of Russia ; and H. I. and R. H. the Archduke of Austria.

This is the only Hotel in India at which H. R. H. The Princess of Wales stayed during the Royal Tour.

This Hotel is unsurpassed for its excellence of cuisine and accommodation ; it is the **Largest and Most Select Hotel in India,** replete with every modern addition and improvement, and situated in the healthiest part of Mussoorie, overlooking the Happy Valley and **Facing the Snows.**

And is entirely under the
Personal Supervision of the Proprietors.

Magnificent Ballroom, Ladies' Drawingroom, Spacious Smoking and Cardroom and Billiard room, with two tables, also Post, Telephone and Telegraph Office on the premises.

The Charleville String Band, specially engaged for the whole season, plays during dinner each evening.

Bachelors' Quarters are unequalled in comfort, view and excellence of accommodation.

An advertisement of Charleville Hotel in 1908. Advertisement mentions the ballroom, card room and billiard room while also mentioning the name and credentials of the proprietor Wultzer. It also refers to the post office on the hotel premises. (Source: Kinney T., The Echo Guide to Mussoorie, Mussoorie: Echo Press, 1908)

limited liability company 'Wultzer Ltd' in 1906—and for several years, handsome dividends were paid to the shareholders. 'The Charleville Hotel flourishes and prospers in every-increasing proportion,' noted Bodycot[268] (1907) in his guidebook.

The Criterion Restaurant, at present-day Gandhi Chowk (where Imperial Restaurant is now located) was also purchased by Wultzer in 1885. This German did have some business acumen. Under his management, The Criterion too became one of the finest restaurants in town. Every evening, the army band played at the band stand, right opposite The Criterion, which further added to the charm of the place.

Post-independence, the Government of India acquired this splendid estate to set up a training academy for the civil servants. The 'babus' always seem to get the best of everything, don't they?

Charleville was lost in the sands of time, and so was the seal of the post office in the hotel premises, which changed from 'Charleville' to 'NAA' (after the National Academy of Administration). The academy was later renamed Lal Bahadur Shastri National Academy of Administration (LBSNAA) after the late prime minister.

The last vestige of Charleville was destroyed in 1984 when a devastating fire consumed the original building of Charleville and, along with it, a treasure trove of old books and documents maintained in the library of LBSNAA. But old memories etched in time seldom fade away. Ask any old timer—sadly, they are also few and far between—and they still refer to this place as Charleville.

The people of Mussoorie hold a grudge against Kipling because, while he wrote verses upon verses about Shimla, he failed to write anything of substance about our town. But he did immortalize Wultzer and his Charleville hotel through a couplet:

> And there were men with thousand wants
> And women with babes galore-
> But the dear little angels in heaven know
> That Wultzer never swore.

---

[268]Bodycot F., *Guide to Mussoorie* (Mussoorie: Mafasilite Printing Works, 1907), 11.

The Savoy

Few years ago, a friend who was staying at The Savoy came over for dinner. Elated by the property, he declared, 'If Mussoorie bears the title of the Queen of the Hills, I designate Savoy as the King of Hotels!' Such is the rustic charm of this historic hotel that has been in existence since 1902 and has recently been renovated.

Cecil D. Lincoln, an Irish barrister from Lucknow, purchased the 20-acre estate of the Masuri Seminary School (also known as Maddock's School and Stoke's School) and transformed it into a grand hotel. 'The Savoy hotel has sprung, phoenix-like, from the ashes of the Mussoorie school,' observed Bodycot[269] (1907).

A view of Hotel Savoy (circa 1950). Noticeable are the chateau style round towers bordering the building. (Photo courtesy: Hotel Savoy, Mussoorie)

---

[269]Ibid.

Savoy Hotel (French: *savoie*) was ostensibly named after the famous Savoy Hotel of central London (1889). I would have left the matter here—after all, 'What's in a name?'—had I not stumbled upon a book by Elaine Denby[270] (1998) that indicates that the name 'Savoy' is linked to medieval French history. One thing led to another until I realized that the name 'Savoy' has a 2,000-year-old history.

Readers, I feel compelled to share this interesting bit with you. A peek into history takes us more than two millennia ago, to the age of the warlike Gauls. Who can forget the iconic characters, Asterix and Obelix, who managed to beat the Roman army into a pulp in every comic book of Goscinny's?

A region in western-Alps, under the occupation of the Gauls, was referred as Sapaudia (Gaulish meaning 'fir'). Humbert occupied this region around 1000 AD and established the 'County of Savoy'. Peter II, a descendant of Humbert, built the Savoy Palace in London between the Strand and River Thames.[271] In 1880, the famous Savoy Theatre was built on the grounds of the former palace by impresario Richard D'Oyly Carte. The luxurious Savoy Hotel, to which Mussoorie's Savoy owes its name, was constructed adjoining the theatre.

No wonder Lincoln, the founder of The Savoy at Mussoorie, made a conscious effort to recreate the palatial French chateaus of the sixteenth century in the Chateausque[272] style of architecture[273]: the two round towers bordering each building of the main block; a large courtyard with a grandiose staircase leading up to the

---

[270]Denby E., *Grand Hotels* (London: Reaktion Books Ltd, 1998), 143.

[271]'European Kingdoms', *The History Files*, www.historyfiles.co.uk/KingLists Europe/ItalySavoy.htm

[272]'Chateauesque Style 1860–1910', *Pennsylvania Historical & Museum Commission*, www.phmc.state.pa.us/portal/communities/architecture/styles/chateauesque.html.

[273]This style of architecture is a potpourri of architectural motifs, borrowing from both the Gothic and Renaissance styles.

main building; bay windows on the outer walls and lancet shaped windows inside the building, they all seem to carry the visitors into medieval France. Since the iconic building is designed like a French chateau, perhaps a more befitting name for this grand hotel is 'Chateau de Savoy'!

Savoy boasted of large and spacious suites; 'spinster's quarters' and 'bachelor's quarters' to cater to unmarried or unaccompanied ladies and gentlemen; 'a large dining saloon, a fine drawing room, reading room, billiard room with two tables, card room and the bar.'[274]

Savoy's bar, now referred to as the 'writer's bar', is perhaps the most famous bar in town—a wall adorns plaques bearing the names of famous 'writers' (authors) who visited the hotel over the years (or had any association with the hotel or the town) starting from Mussoorie's own Ruskin Bond, Rudyard Kipling, Pearl S. Buck, John Lang, Jim Corbett and Lowell Thomas to name a few.

Liquor was consumed profusely at the bar, and Lincoln, the owner, made every drop count. The empty bottles were collected in the cellar where dregs were painstakingly drained out and two full bottles were ready the next day for the house guests.[275]

Savoy excelled in hospitality for its guests, ably aided in this endeavour by the manager F. Schmuck, a German with wide experience of the hospitality industry. Schmuck had worked for some of the most distinguished personalities of his era, including the Prince and Princess of Wales and the Viceroy of India.[276]

To cater to the pallets of the gourmet, Savoy had its own dairy; a piggery with 'English pigs'; a poultry farm; an orchard of exotic fruits from France; an extensive vegetable garden in

---

[274]Kinney T., *The Echo Guide to Mussoorie* (Mussoorie: Echo Press, 1908), 93.

[275]Misra P.R., 'Mussoorie: The pleasure capital of yore', *The Times of India*, 15 December 2015, https://timesofindia.indiatimes.com/city/dehradun/Mussoorie-The-pleasure-capital-of-yore/articleshow/50058248.cms

[276]Kinney T., *The Echo Guide to Mussoorie* (Mussoorie: Echo Press, 1908), 93.

which specially selected asparagus was cultivated; and, to top it all, a specially constructed 'quaillery'.[277]

A fine orchestra, a ballroom full of couples, belly dancers, cabaret dancers and fancy dress parties kept the blithesome and sometimes unconstrained visitors busy, night after night. A 'separation bell' had to be invented to avoid scandals (see chapter 8).

Brisk business done by The Criterion Café prompted Savoy to set up its café on the first floor of the Mussoorie Library building. As the army band played in the evenings, Englishmen and English women immaculately attired in evening dresses thronged The Savoy Café.

A grand legacy of Savoy is the post office housed inside the hotel premises since 1902, which is still operational with a century old seal and a print of 'Savoy Hotel'; perhaps the only functional post office in the country today to be housed inside a hotel and to bear the seal of the hotel.

Mussoorie has produced hockey players of international repute, but tennis at 6,000 feet? Believe me, one of the earliest tennis tournaments of India—the UP[278] Hard Court Tennis Championship—was organized in Mussoorie and hosted at Savoy since the early 1930s.[279] The tournament was of such a scale and repute that it attracted the best players from across the country; the roll of honours features legends such as Ghaus Mohammad (first Indian to reach the quarter finals at Wimbledon) and Ramanathan Krishnan (two times semi-finalist at Wimbledon). This tourney continued till the 1980s.

Tennis reminds me of the Gaekwads of Baroda, who would book an entire block of Savoy adjoining the tennis courts for the convenience of the royal ladies (who loved to play the sport).

---

[277] Ibid.

[278] Uttar Pradesh

[279] It is believed that this tournament was first started in Happy Valley Club, Mussoorie, and later moved to Savoy.

Savoy's magic has attracted a fair share of royalty, starting from the visit by the Princess of Wales, who attended a garden party here in 1906; the Afghan conference in 1920, where British and Afghan officials came to the negotiation table after the third Anglo-Afghan war when, it is believed, the British asked Pt. Jawaharlal Nehru to leave the Savoy premises lest he should stir discontent among the Afghans.

Like the Gaekwads, the Wadiyars of Mysore were also known to take over entire blocks. The Shah of Iran, King of Nepal, Emperor of Ethiopia, Crown Prince of Laos and the Prince of Cambodia were amongst the royalty from foreign nations that stayed at The Savoy.

In 1946, Rai Bahadur Kripa Ram (or Captain Kripa Ram) of Karachi bought the Savoy from Lincoln. His family continued to operate the Savoy for over half a century, although Savoy's fortunes dipped post-independence and gradually, the property went into disrepair. Perhaps the mounting losses or difficulty in maintaining such a huge property prompted Mr Anand Jauhar (son of Captain Kripa Ram) to part with several chunks of the erstwhile 20-acre estate.

Finally, Savoy was sold to its present owners, Mr K.K. Kaya and Mr R.P. Singh, in 2005. By that time, the run-down Savoy was merely a shadow of its former self. The hotel was painstakingly restored and reopened in 2013, and the 'Savoy Magic' lives on.

Hakman's Grand Hotel

While Savoy and Charleville were known for splendour and luxury, Hakman's was the entertainment hub of the town.

Mr Saul Hakman, a German hairdresser, was the proprietor of this hotel. In the early 1900s, he ran his hair dressing saloon in the South End building on the Mall. In a couple of decades, the Jew was able to amass sufficient wealth to build this iconic hotel. Its prominent location on the Mall made it easily accessible and hence quite popular as an evening sojourn.

It was a happening place where plays, circuses, dance and musical performances were organized every evening. I have read accounts of the famous magician Gogia Pasha performing here in the 1940s while the legendary tenor saxophone[280] player Rudy Cotton's[281] band enthralled the audience for decades with their jazz music. Sensual Greata, with her snake dance routine, and Jeanne Carrol, with her circus troupe, drew large crowds to the hotel. And if this was not enough, there was 'dance and cabaret' every evening.

While passing Hakman's, it was a ritual to steal a glance at the posters of cabaret artists put up on the gate of the hotel. Many parents went to the extent of commanding their teenage sons to look straight ahead while passing these gates.

And then there was the Palladium Cinema (later Capitol Cinema) on the ground floor of Hakman's, thronged by English movie buffs.

Mr Hakman died in 1932, and Mrs Hakman continued his legacy until she decided to wind up in 1946. Mrs Hakman promptly issued a notice in the local papers asking all creditors to settle their accounts by 15 July 1946.[282]

The subsequent owners did well until the late 1970s when rising entertainment taxes and decline in the audience forced Hakman's out of business. With the ball room and the cinema

---

[280]Tenor saxophone is a medium-sized saxophone that is commonly used as a solo instrument in jazz music.

[281]Rudy Cotton (birth name Cawas Khatau) was a Parsi saxophone player who is regarded as one of the greatest tenor saxophone players of Indian origin—he had a large fan following that included former Attorney General of India, the late Shri Soli Sorabjee. Rudy died in Delhi in 1985. His band performed at Hakman's for several decades, starting from the mid-1940s. His band included Pat Blake, Danny Salvador and Frank Fernand on trumpets, Johnny Gomes on alto, Solo Jacobs on piano, Carl Evans on bass and Leslie Weekes on drums.

[282]*The Mussoorie Advertiser*, 1946, Vol 4, No. 11, Mussoorie: Mussoorie Art Press.

hall closed, only hotel rooms were available, although they also went into disrepair.

Even after a century, this magnificent two-story building still manages to stand tall, reminding one and all of its past glory. Some time back it had been taken over by developers from New Delhi. I am keeping my fingers crossed that in their zeal to redo the building, they do not end up killing the nostalgic charm and aura of the grand old Hakman's.

The great bargain

The story of Hakman's would be incomplete without making a mention of a certain British soldier or 'Tommy' who had made a 'great bargain' at the gates of Palladium Cinema.

One evening, the Tommy hired a rickshaw to take him to the cinema. Upon reaching his destination, the Tommy asked the rickshaw puller, '*Kitna paisa?* (How much?)'

'*Barah anna*[283] (Twelve anna),' replied the rickshaw man.

Our Tommy, who apparently had arrived in India recently and knew little Hindi, felt that '12' was a very big number.

'Darn it!' the Tommy retorted. 'Do you think I am a rajah?'

'*Yeh lo ek rupiya.* (Here, take one rupee.)' Tommy threw a rupee coin, smiled smugly and promptly marched into Palladium Cinema.

It was a good bargain for the Tommy and for the rickshaw puller!

Mr X's first drink at Hakman's

There have been plenty of incidents wherein inebriated British gentlemen engaged in all sorts of revelry in our town. Not to be left behind, the Indian tipplers, too, have had their fair share of

---

[283]One anna equals 6.25 paise and twelve anna equals 75 paise.

boisterous and notorious acts. This is a real story of a resident—in fact a popular politician of the town—who simply wanted to have a drink at the Hakman's while enjoying the music.

It was a fine evening in the summer of 1978 when a young Mr X (as the protagonist forbade me to use even the initials of his name), then in his early twenties, who was already a student leader of some repute.

Tall and burly, Mr X was a well-known personality. The good natured and carefree Mr X was fond of his drinks and was a bit of a reveler in those days.

That fateful evening, after a few drinks, he ventured on the Mall Road and reached Jhoola Ghar, just before Hakman's, and spotted a horse; until 2012, horse owners with their horses in tow roamed around the town, offering rides on rent.

'Come here,' Mr X beckoned a horse owner.

And within seconds, Mr X had 'boarded' the horse and off he went towards Library, his horse at a brisk trot. Mall Road was bustling with tourists who scampered out of the way.

As Mr X was returning towards Jhoola Ghar, he heard the sound of melodious music from Hakman's; it drowned out the clopping of his horse on the pavement.

'I have never had a drink at Hakman's, nor have I heard their orchestra,' Mr X thought, and instinctively turned his horse towards the entrance of the hotel.

The old gatekeeper at Hakman's had, over the years, dealt with many gora sahebs in various states of intoxication, but never before had a tippler charged at him on a horse.

Scared out of his wits, he reluctantly put his hand out and had barely shouted, '*Ruk jao!* (Wait!)' when a kick from our hero knocked him out.

There is a flight of half-a-dozen stairs at the entrance, and notwithstanding the low-roof, our Mr X ducked and clung—Clint Eastwood style—to the mane of the horse—as if evading imaginary bullets that whizzed past his head.

His arrival in the dining room created mayhem. Ladies and gents ran helter-skelter, the orchestra disappeared, waiters carrying food and drinks dove for cover over the sound of crashing dishes. As Mr X and his horse stopped smack in the centre of the large dining hall, it was empty save for the manager who, paralysed with fear, was rooted in a corner.

Recognizing Mr X as a mischief maker and a reveler, the scared manager stepped forward.

'How can I help you, sir?' he managed to whisper.

'I need a drink,' was the calm reply as our reveler alighted from his horse and occupied a table.

'Certainly, sir. What would you prefer?'

'Your best scotch! A large peg,' Mr X thundered. 'Where is your orchestra? I want to hear them play,' he demanded.

So the drink was brought and, hurriedly, the orchestra was organized to give a solo performance for the benefit of our hero.

'Cheque, please,' Mr X boomed after finishing his drink. 'My ride?' he queried as he stood up after paying for his drink.

'It's waiting outside, sir,' the poor manager stammered.

'Bring my ride here, right now,' our hero ordered.

So the horse made another entry into the dining room, and Mr X calmly rode it out of Hakman's.

12

BANKING IN THE HILLS

For the rustic British-era hill town of Mussoorie, the word 'bank' has more connotations than that of a mere financial institution. This term is inextricably linked to the names of various old buildings of British, Irish or Scottish origin. These settlers added the word 'bank' to the name of their properties. So we have a Waverley Bank, a Bothwell Bank and a Laurel Bank, all named after places in England, Scotland and Ireland, respectively. We also have houses named after flowers—Rose Bank, Dahlia Bank, Violet Bank, Ivy Bank and Thistle Bank. But some of the more imaginative residents named their houses after fruits, so we even have a Raspberry Bank and a Strawberry Bank here.

But speaking about banks per se, starting from the year 1840, our town has had its fair share of banks.[284] It is another matter that almost all banks that opened shop here collapsed like a house of cards, bringing promoters, shareholders and even depositors to grief.

North-West Bank (formerly Mussoori Bank)

It so happened that the first bank to come up was named after our town—the Mussoori Bank. It was floated by Colonel F. Angelo, Mr Solaroli and Mr Troop in January 1840, with a

---

[284]Banking finds references in Vedic literature. The Manusmriti speaks of deposits, pledges, loans and interest rates while records of money lending are also found during the reign of Mauryan kings. However, institutionalized banking in India is credited to the British, and The Bank of Hindustan (1790) was the first banking institution of the country.

share capital of ₹50,000. In 1841, seven more shareholders were roped in, and the bank restyled into a joint stock bank with a capital of ₹5 lakhs (Rao, 1982[285]). It was later rechristened as North-West Bank.

The bank was accused of irregular dealings; following an enquiry in 1851, irregularities amounting to ₹130,000 were discovered. The bank went into liquidation in 1859, with shareholders managing to get ₹182 per share.

The Delhi and London Bank Ltd

Headquartered in London, this bank was established in India in 1844. It had branches in Calcutta, Delhi and Lucknow, and was introduced to Mussoorie in 1859[286] and, several years later, in Shimla. Imagine our dear little town at par with these large cities! The bank had a subscribed capital of around £337,625 in 1884.[287] Indian branches of the bank were merged with the Alliance Bank of Simla in 1916.[288] The head office of the bank was located at Chandni Chowk in New Delhi, where a branch of the State Bank of India is housed presently.

Mussoorie Bank Ltd (formerly Mussoorie Savings Bank)

Mussoorie Savings Bank was a purely local bank constituted in 1864 by Mr Hobson[289] with Colonel C.G. Barlow. It was later constituted

---

[285]Rao E.G.K., 'Development of Banking Institutions in India in the Eighteenth-Nineteenth Century', *Indian Journal of History of Science*, Vol. 17, No. 1, 1982, 91–113.
[286]Northam J., *Guide to Masuri, Landaur, Dehradun and The Hills North of Dehra* (Calcutta: Thacker, Spink and Co., 1884), 34.
[287]Ibid, 201.
[288]Jones G., *British Multinational Banking, 1830–1990* (UK: Clarendon Press, 1995), 407.
[289]Bodycot F., *Guide to Mussoorie* (Mussoorie: Mafasilite Printing Works, 1907), 33.

into a joint stock bank and renamed 'Mussoorie Bank Ltd' with paid-up capital of ₹3 lakhs. It disappeared in the early 1900s.[290]

MUSSOORIE BANK LIMITED.

ESTABLISHED MAY 1864.

Incorporated with Limited Liability, under Act VII, 1860.

Trustees:

Colonel C. G. Barlow. | G. H. Coates, Esq.

PAID-UP CAPITAL, Rs. 3,00,000.

HEAD OFFICE ... ... MUSSOORIE.

Bills drawn on the Union Bank of London.

The Bank grants and purchases Bills on London and Drafts on Calcutta, Bombay, Allahabad, Cawnpore, Bareilly, Shahjehanpore, Lucknow, Agra, Meerut, Roorkee, Saharunpore, Delhi, Umballa, Rawul Pindee, Simla, Nynee Tal, Lahore, Jullundur, Mooltan, and Chuckratta.

Government Securities bought and sold.
Loans and Cash Credits granted on approved security.

FLOATING DEPOSITS received repayable on demand, on Cheques of not less than Rs. 10. No Interest allowed, nor any charge made.

INTEREST DEPOSITS.

On sums deposited, Interest will be allowed as follows:
6 per cent. requiring 12 months' notice of withdrawal.

5	"	"	9	"	"
4	"	"	6	"	"
3	"	"	4	"	"

Special Home Remittance Deposits, requiring 2 years' notice of withdrawal. Interest at 5 per cent., Interest payable half-yearly by this Bank's Bills on London at 2 Shillings per Rupee, without accumulative effect.

2nd. Ordinary Home remittance Deposits.—Interest allowed on these Deposits at 4 per cent. for this Bank's Bill on London, without any previous notice, at exchange of the day.

The Bank reserves to itself the right of closing any of the above deposits, or of modifying the terms, on giving one month's notice.

All communications to be addressed, and remittances made payable, to "The Manager, Mussoorie Bank, Limited. Hours of business, 10 A.M. to 4 P.M. On Saturdays, 10 A.M. to 1 P.M.

G. H. WEBB, *Manager.*

An advertisement of Mussoorie bank that appeared in an 1884 guidebook. The bank came to grief in the early twentieth century. (Source: Northam J., Guide to Masuri, Landaur, Dehradun and The Hills North of Dehra, Calcutta: Thacker, Spink and Co., 1884, 185)

Himalaya Bank

This bank began operations in 1874 from a splendid building on the Mall where Himalaya Hotel was earlier housed. Owned by Mr F. Moss (after whom Mossy falls has been named) the bank did

[290]Ibid.

exceedingly well in the initial years, prompting Northam[291] (1884) to write that the bank had made 'such progress as to render it a firmly established institution'.

Soon, fortunes turned for Mr Moss and his bank was liquidated shortly after. The Alliance Bank of Simla was appointed as the liquidator of Himalaya Bank, which prompted the bank to open a branch at Mussoorie.

Bank of Upper India opened its branch in this building but the bank failed and subsequently a branch of the Imperial Bank of India (which later became the State Bank of India) was established here.

HIMALAYA BANK, LIMITED.

Capital, Rs. 2,00,000.

HEAD OFFICE, MUSSÓORIE.

London Bankers: UNION BANK OF LONDON.

Bills drawn and purchased on London at the current rates of exchange. Bills for and under £10 can only be granted on demand. Bills for less than £50 are not issued at longer usance than three months.

The Bank will transmit, free of charge (except for postage), the First of Exchange direct, on being furnished with the correct address of the addressee.

Drafts bought and sold on Calcutta, Madras, Bombay, Allahabad, Lahore, Benares, Cawnpore, Lucknow, Agra, Meerut, Delhi, Roorkee, Saharunpore, Simla, Nynee Tal, Murree, Rawalpindi, Umbala, Mooltan, Jubbulpore, and all the principal stations in India.

Fixed Deposits are now received on the following terms:—

$$\left.\begin{array}{c} 6 \\ 5 \\ 4 \\ 3 \end{array}\right\} \text{per cent. per annum,} \left.\begin{array}{c} 12 \text{ months'} \\ 9 \\ 6 \\ 3 \end{array}\right\} \text{notice of withdrawal.}$$

The above deposits may generally be availed of without notice by the Bank's Bills on London. The Bank reserves to itself the right, on giving one month's notice, of paying off any of the above deposits, or of modifying its terms.

Current Accounts are also received and kept without charge.

LOANS AND CASH CREDITS are granted on the security of Government Paper, Bank and other joint stock shares, mortgages on approved personal securities, on the usual terms.

GOVERNMENT PAPER and other securities purchased, sold, and kept in safe custody, at the usual charge of ¼ per cent. For further particulars, apply to the Manager.

Remittances to be endorsed thus—"Pay to the Himalaya Bank, Limited, or order."

HOURS OF BUSINESS, 10 to 4. Saturday, 10 to 2.

F. MOSS, *Manager.*

An advertisement of Himalaya Bank that appeared in an 1884 guidebook. (Source: Northam J., Guide to Masuri, Landaur, Dehradun and The Hills North of Dehra, Calcutta: Thacker, Spink and Co., 1884, 173)

---

[291]Northam J., *Guide to Masuri, Landaur, Dehradun and The Hills North of Dehra* (Calcutta: Thacker, Spink and Co., 1884), 34.

Bank of Upper India

Founded in Meerut in 1862, it has the distinction of being the first joint stock bank of India. It has branches in Agra, Lucknow, Allahabad (now Prayagraj), Bareilly, Delhi, Shimla, Nainital and Mussoorie. The Mussoorie branch was opened in the 1870s but closed shortly afterwards and reopened in 1904 in the premises of the Himalaya Hotel.[292] This bank, too, failed in 1913.

Even after the closure of the Bank of Upper India, prolonged litigation followed with Robert Hercules Skinner—a scion of the illustrious Skinner family of Mussoorie—regarding some properties of the Skinner family mortgaged with the bank. This was settled in 1942.

Alliance Bank of Simla

This was established in 1874 in Shimla (Simla, as it was known then) by Sir James Lewis Walker. With thirty-six branches, it was once regarded amongst the successful banks of British India.

A view of the lower Mall (circa 1912). Tiverton House can be seen towards the right.

[292]Bodycot F., *Guide to Mussoorie* (Mussoorie: Mafasilite Printing Works, 1907), 33.

Several sick banks that were operating in Mussoorie were taken over by the Alliance Bank, including Himalaya Bank; Delhi and London Bank; and Bank of Upper India.

The Alliance Bank of Simla started operations at Mussoorie on, '21st August 1891 in very handsome premises known as the Tiverton House at the east end of the Mall.'[293] After a successful innings, Alliance Bank ran into troubled waters due to 'speculative investments' made by the management. The bank was closed and many of its properties were sold, while some were taken over by the Imperial Bank (as Imperial Bank had paid fifty per cent liabilities of Alliance Bank).

Tiverton House presently houses the Allahabad Bank (or the Indian Bank, as it is called now).

The Imperial Bank of India (IBI)

Established in 1921, the Imperial Bank of India set up shop in Mussoorie in the 1920s in the same premises where the Himalaya Bank once operated. Post-independence, it became the State Bank of India in 1955; the main branch of the State Bank of India was housed on the ground floor of this building.

The names of former managers were mentioned on a 'roll of honour' inside the manager's chamber. Was there a historian hiding among the lot of bookkeepers? But thanks to the unknown benefactor, we were able to get a peek into history. Among these names, I found the name of Mr S.C. Choudhury, the father of General Shankar Roychowdhury, our 18th Army Chief.

Managers at this branch had the entire first floor as their residence—perhaps the best accommodation available to any bank manager in India. I remember visiting this expansive residence and being amazed by the antique furniture, the splendid verandah overlooking the Mall with wrought-iron railings of Victorian era

---

[293]Ibid.

with the letters 'VI' (meaning Victoria Imperatrix) moulded into the railing.

The bank's premises came to be owned by Life Insurance Corporation (LIC) of India, and a feisty litigation ensued for decades. Finally, LIC managed to gain possession of the building.

Mansa Ram Bank

This bank was owned by an Indian businessman from Saharanpur, Mr Mansa Ram. Started in the 1920s, the bank had its head office in Dehradun with branches in Mussoorie, Saharanpur and Haridwar. In Mussoorie, the branch was in Landour.

Mr Mansa Ram owned extensive property in Mussoorie, including the famous Mullingar Building. Mansaram Cricket was a small ground near Mullingar, also owned by this businessman—and although the ground has been replaced by rows of houses, the locality is still called Mansaram Cricket.

He is also credited with constructing the Connaught Place in Dehradun. It's a three-storeyed residential complex with over a hundred flats and commercial spaces at Chakrata Road in Dehradun, thereby prompting the scions of the royal family of Nepal, Shanta Shumsher Jung Bahadur Rana and Colonel Shashi Shumsher Jung Bahadur Rana, who had their residence at Fair Lawn Estate in Mussoorie, to build an equally grand complex adjoining the Connaught Place.

The banker defaulted on his loan from Bharat Insurance Company as his project failed to take off. The company took over his complex, and it is under the ownership of LIC today.

His bank, too, failed and went into liquidation in 1955. However, his family still owns property in Mussoorie.

Tiverton House

The worn down, two-storeyed building located bang opposite the ropeway on the Mall Road is the Tiverton House.

A recent picture of the Tiverton House. The building still retains much of its old charm although the interiors are in a state of disrepair.

'In its heydays it must have been the mansion of a rich British Lord,' I once overheard a tourist make this casual remark.

He may have been right. This grand building, with an arched verandah on the ground floor and large bay windows on the first floor, has a regal appearance. Sadly, zealous perusal of old guide books and journals did not throw up any names of a purported British Lord who resided here.

The earliest record that I managed to retrieve dates to 1891, when a branch of Alliance Bank of Simla was opened here. My great-grandfather, after he migrated to Mussoorie in 1901, worked as an assistant manager in this bank, until racist abuse by the branch manager prompted him to strike the manager with a ruler (a thick wooden baton used as a scale) and walk out of the building. 'My father had forbid me from ever visiting this bank,' my grandfather remarked while narrating this incident.

After the liquidation of Alliance Bank of Simla, a branch of Allahabad Bank opened at this building. As luck would have it, in 1960, my father joined Allahabad Bank with his first posting at Mussoorie.

'Get another job, you will not work in these premises,' my grandfather thundered.

'The British have long gone; it is our people managing this bank now,' my father pleaded. 'And don't forget, in response to the racial abuse, your father had broken the head of the gora. Wasn't that redemption enough?' he added, and was finally able to convince my grandfather.

As a kid, I have fond memories of visiting the premises and stuffing my tiny pockets with peaches, plums, pears and apricots that grew in the bank compound.

'*Chote bhaiya, aur le lo* (little brother, take more),' the generous gardener would urge.

I would spend hours gazing at a pair of goldfish in a small pool in the garden. A large black safe in my father's chamber once caught my fancy. 'This safe is more than a hundred-years-old, manufactured by world famous Chubb company of UK,' my father once informed.

A few years ago, I happened to bump into our local tehsildar Mr Puran Singh, and one thing led to another until I found out that his father used to work as a gardener at Allahabad Bank. 'Dahlias and chrysanthemums grown by my father used to win first prize in the flower show at the Savoy Hotel,' he beamed.

A small world indeed!

The branch of Allahabad Bank is still operational at this run-down building. The large garden does exist, but the prize-winning flowers have disappeared. A few fruit trees are visible, but I have not noticed any kids around. The goldfish, I am told, were devoured by a cat years ago and were never reintroduced.

Will the bank authorities ever restore the glory of Tiverton House? I doubt it.

The guard who caught a wink once too often

Amongst those that feature in the honours list at State Bank (Imperial Bank when this incident occurred) was a British manager who was a strict disciplinarian. For quite some time, he had been receiving reports that the night duty guard was dozing off during his shift. 'He is sleeping most of the time, even a child can come and rob your bank,' said a neighbour.

The manager was furious! He contemplated reprimanding the errant guard, but decided to wait for an opportune moment.

One evening, oblivious of these developments, the guard reported for duty. With a gun on his shoulder, he started making rounds of the arched verandah outside the entrance of the bank. Around 7 p.m., the manager returned from his customary walk, nodded to the guard and went up to his residence on the first floor.

'He will not come down till morning,' thought the guard as he took the gun off his shoulder, settled down in a chair just outside the gate of the bank, and placed his gun alongside the chair. 'This is a useless job, sitting out in the cold,' he muttered as he retrieved a quilt from behind the chair and covered himself. For good measure, he also pulled out a small bottle of country-liquor and took a few sips. Soon he was fast asleep, snoring gently.

In the middle of the night, the manager tiptoed down the stairs of this residence and carefully sneaked up on the guard. He was furious upon finding the guard fast asleep on his watch. But he had already thought of a fitting plan to punish the errant watchman. Gently, he picked up the gun and carried it to his residence, careful not to make a noise.

The nip of the liquor and the warmth of the quilt ensured that the guard had a good night's sleep. As he rose out of his slumber, he realized that his gun was missing.

He frantically searched for the gun, but in vain. Fear and panic gripped him.

'Oh God! The gora saheb will surely kill me,' he thought.

In the morning, he waited with baited breath for the branch manager; with shaky legs, he reached the manager's chamber and reported the loss of the gun.

'How can anyone take away your gun? You are a strong man and trained in physical combat. Why did you not shoot the intruder?' the manager questioned.

'Sorry, sir, I was asleep when my gun went missing,' the guard replied in a hoarse voice.

'Sleeping! Are you paid to sleep on your watch? I will hand you over to the police,' boomed the manager.

By this time the harried guard was prostrate before the manager.

'Sir, this will never happen again. Please hit me, abuse me, but do not hand me to the police.'

The manager told him to go to his quarter and come back in the evening.

As the guard returned in the evening for his duty, he found the manager standing at the gate of the bank holding the gun that was 'stolen'.

'Here's your gun. The police found it with a thief who had crept up on you and stole it. Imagine a guard of the Imperial Bank, my guard, looted by a petty thief!' the manager said belligerently.

The poor guard stood with folded hands. He was shaking with fear and tears were rolling down his cheeks. The manager ordered the guard to resume his duty and admonished that he should not make any mistakes again.

Many months later, the manager narrated the entire incident to his friends.

'I have never found him sleeping on his watch again. It seems this trick worked. The guard still believes that a thief sneaked up on him,' the manager chuckled, taking a sip of the fine scotch that his friends had brought for him.

13

THE SAGA OF THE SILVER SCREEN

One evening, as I returned from work, a huge crowd had gathered in the lane that led to my house. Hundreds of people thronged that narrow lane—tourists, hotel staff, shopkeepers, women and children—all seemed to be intently gazing towards the Tilak Library located there.

Something's amiss, I thought as my journalistic instincts took over and I tried to push past the crowd. But no one seemed to budge an inch. Amidst the clamour I thought I heard someone shout 'shooting'. This set alarm bells ringing.

I sprinted up the staircase of an SBI branch nearby, pushing past the guard who tried to block my way.

'*Woh raha, woh raha* (there he is, there he is),' came the roar from the crowd as I watched from my vantage point our action hero, John Abraham, emerging from Tilak Library. He was shooting for *Batla House* (2019), I was later told.

Actually, I am a bit of a 'pro' at watching film shoots. *Ghar Ka Chiragh* (1989) was my first. When Raj Kumar starrer *Police Public* (1990) was shot here, our school principal had turned the director away, 'This is a school not a film studio,' he had admonished. But I cannot forget the late-night wait near the GPO on the Mall where the legendary actor's shot was scheduled—everyone in the impatient crowd was imitating the inimitable actor's famous dialogue, 'Jaani...'

My town has so much to attract filmmakers: serene surroundings, fascinating views, waterfalls, heritage buildings. Thus, *Teesri Manzil* (1966), *Dulhan Ek Raat Ki* (1967), *Pardesi* (1970), *Anhonee* (1973), *Karm* (1977), *Armaan* (2003), *Shivaay* (2016), *Kabir Singh* (2019), *Student of the Year 2* (2019) are a few more films that I can recall that have been shot here, not to name the numerous television serials, advertisements and other cinematic ventures.

Our Own Film Stars

Mussoorie has its own star cast, too, comprising of some great actors.

Son of the soil, the late Tom Alter saheb, has left behind plenty of bittersweet memories. 'I get roles because there is no other angrez who can speak fluent Hindi and recite Urdu poetry,' he modestly maintained, but who can undermine his genius and unforgettable roles in *Kranti* (1981), the Urdu-loving Captain Weston in *Shatranj Ke Khiladi* (1977) or the strict hotel warden in *Aashiqui* (1990). I cannot forget the humorous 'kissas' that he narrated—every time he seemed to have a new one. When his childhood friend (from Mussoorie) found himself behind bars, Tom saheb rushed to visit him in jail and ended up spending two hours with the movie-buff jailor.

'*Jailor ne film ki script likhi thi, behad vahiyat, par mujhe sunni padi, khoob wah wah bhi karni padi kyonki dost jail mein tha* (Jailor had written an absolute rubbish script for a film, but I had to listen to it and even praise it because my friend was in jail),' he narrated after his jail visit.

When we met next, he told me that his friend had started getting good treatment inside the jail.

'But the jailor keeps on asking when will Tom Alter visit again. I am afraid if I visit again, he might decide to lock me up so that he can get a "captive" audience,' Tom saheb quipped.

The affable and most down-to-earth Bollywood and Hollywood star Victor Banerjee has made Mussoorie his second home since the 1980s. He has a beautiful house in Landour called The Parsonage. There were several incidents of fire in his house, until Victor sir's daughter drew a painting of the Goddess of Fire just outside the gate. Lucky charm? The humble Mr Banerjee is often spotted driving up and down the Mullingar slope. Readers, next time you visit, be on the lookout for an off-white Getz car, you might meet the man himself.

The late Prem Nath and Bina Roy owned Kailash Cottage in Landour (the actress had inherited this house) and were regular visitors till 1990. A piece of trivia—the maid that worked with them also worked at our house. '*Prem Nath saheb to bas baithe-baithe khaate rehte hai* (Prem Nath sir just sits and eats); she once told my mom.

Filmmaker Vishal Bhardwaj has also built his summer nest in Landour, right next to Ruskin Bond's house. Bhardwaj has adapted two stories of the octogenarian author into films: *Blue Umbrella* (2005) and *7 Khoon Maaf* (2011).

The elegant Jaya Prada's husband owns the Nahata Estate at Lal Tibba—but the actress maintains a fair distance from our town—wonder why?

Then we have former students who made it to stardom. The dapper Kanwaljit Singh and the soulful Lucky Ali are both from St. George's College. I have fond memories of chatting with them over dinners. The eloquent Saeed Jaffrey, who passed away in 2015, was another illustrious alumnus who studied at both St. George's and Wynberg Allen. Wynberg Allen alumni will not forgive me if I fail to put in a word about their alumnus, the stylish Meiyang Chang or the muscular Nawab Shah.

Cinema Halls

Mussoorie's tryst with cinema goes back to the early 1900s, the 'silent era' of cinema, when movies without dialogues were in vogue, when on-screen antics of the genius Charlie Chaplin and later, Buster Keaton had the audience in fits; or when classics such as *The Birth of a Nation* (1915), *Cleopatra* (1917), *Oliver Twist* (1922) were immensely popular.

Mussoorie's first movie hall opened in 1912, while two more

came up in the 1920s. Cinema halls in Mussoorie boomed in the 1930s as talking pictures or 'talkies' were vastly popular with the audience. With seven cinema halls, the one-and-a-half kilometre Mall Road was compared to the Broadway Street of US. The British as well as the Indian royalty—revelling at the unofficial 'Pleasure Capital' of the Raj during the summers—thronged the cinema halls.

Picture Palace and Jubilee

It must have been little fun watching movies on a hand-cranked projector where a person manually rotated the projector wheel. The poor audience was at the mercy of the person rotating the wheel, with the movie screen akin to an unbroken horse, that would suddenly bolt ahead or leisurely amble along at times. An ordeal indeed!

'Electric' Picture Palace (1912), the first cinema hall of Mussoorie, was a revelation as its projector was run by electricity and not operated manually. The electric projector was especially imported from Europe, which made it possible for the film to be projected at constant speeds as opposed to the laborious hand-cranked projectors.

And thus, Mussoorie gained the distinction of being only the second town in the country (after Bombay [now Mumbai]) to have an electricity-run cinema.

This iconic movie hall had a café and bar on one side of the hall where a string band played soft music. One could carry alcoholic drinks and tea inside the hall while watching the cinema. Even smoking was permitted. A billiard room entertained those who were not interested in movies. Roaring success and soaring profits prompted the owners to set up the Jubilee Cinema in the basement of Picture Palace in the mid-1930s, making Picture Palace equivalent to a modern-day multiplex.

The 'Electric' Picture Palace in the 1920s. It had a 'ladies lounge and tea room' and also a bar and billiard room. While this building remains more or less the same, the cinema hall has closed long ago. (Picture courtesy: Hotel Savoy, Mussoorie)

Some classics that were run at the cinema include *Sindoor* (1947), which revolved around the social issue of widow remarriage, a 'controversial' issue in the 1940s, and *Dr Kotnis Ki Amar Kahani* (1946), directed by the maestro V. Shantaram, who also played a lead role in the film.

Anand Aur Anand (1984), featuring Dev Anand and his son Suneil Anand, drew huge crowds at the Picture Palace. Suneil and even his sister Devina were alumni of Woodstock School, and the entire school turned up day-after-day for the movie.

I remember watching several movies here during the 1980s and 1990s. But an unforgettable experience was watching the epic horror movie *Evil Dead* (1981), screened here many years after its release. At a late-night show, as the first character in the movie is possessed by demons, a heavy downpour started pounding the roof of the hall, adding further discomfort to the apprehensive audience. Two girls sitting in the front row shrieked with fear, startling my friend D, who also howled. Once the movie ended, I had to walk my scared friend to his house.

'My house is just a minute away. You want me to walk up to Gandhi Chowk and then back. That's nearly 3 kilometres!' I protested.

Finally, his pleadings and even threats to end our friendship made me agree reluctantly.

But the onward journey proved to be most entertaining. During the fifteen-minute walk, I mocked and teased D for his 'cowardice'.

'If you don't have the balls, do not watch horror films. I hope you did not wet your pants,' I taunted.

And poor D, who was the most belligerent of my friends, had his tail between his legs.

After seeing D off, I walked back on the desolate road, hearing the wind murmur softly while an occasional dog howled. As I gazed skywards, a hunchback moon made me uneasy.

Suddenly, the intensity of the wind increased. Above the road, opposite Vasu Cinema, branches of a deodar tree shook vigorously while the oak trees in the compound of Padmini Niwas made loud rustling noises.

'Boy, you're not going bonkers. It is just the wind and the shadows playing with my mind,' I thought.

But fear had already set in. For the next few minutes, every shadow, every silhouette, every tree appeared like a monster to me. As I crossed Garhwal Terrace and approached Hakman's, my mind was haunted by ghost stories of the past. As I reached the gate of Hakman's, a power breakdown (although I still feel it was something else) caused all street lights to go off and the road was plunged into darkness.

I thought I saw a lady standing in the balcony of Hakman's, waving at me and calling my name.

'Oh my God!' I screamed and made a dash towards my house in the dark.

I did not dare stop, did not dare gaze backwards, but puffing and panting, I ran like a madman until my mother opened the door.

While Jubilee closed down in the 1990s, Picture Palace managed to survive the advent of the twenty-first century. This iconic cinema was briefly converted into a 'gaming zone' for kids, along with a 7D theatre and a scary house. But the façade of the building still remains a testament of the glorious 'Electric Picture Palace'.

Rialto

Rialto was, by far, the best movie hall in town in the 1980s and 1990s, and the best part was the 'generous' slope of the floor inside the hall, which allowed an unobstructed view for the audience.

An advertisement of upcoming movies at Rialto in August 1947. The advertisement also announces a 'brand new sound system.' (Source: The Mussoorie Advertiser, 4 August 1947, Vol 5, No. 16. Mussoorie: Mussoorie Art Press)

The origin of this 1936 movie hall is obscure, but readers would be interested to know that there is a 'Cinema Rialto' in Casablanca (built in 1929), Rialto City in California and also a Rialto locality in Venice. So perhaps this name, too, was borrowed, who knows?

Rialto, too, had its fair share of English movies, although Hindi movies were also regularly screened. And after a new sound system was introduced in 1947,[294] the popularity of Rialto increased.

Rialto also had several boxes at the back, although visits from royalty were not as frequent as in Majestic. I have seen a picture of the Tibetan spiritual guru, The Dalai Lama, watching a movie here in 1959–1960.

These 'boxes' were a favourite haunt for love birds who longed for some moments of privacy. There is an interesting story about a well-known and respected gentleman (I am refraining from sharing the name) who had a rendezvous with his girlfriend in the box at Rialto. Someone at the cinema noticed the gentleman and promptly informed his wife—one may call this an advantage or a disadvantage of living in a small town. The movie had barely begun when everyone was startled by the apparition of a lady, holding a sandal in hand, emerging from the shadows and shouting the name of her husband. The poor husband made a bolt for the exit with the lady in hot pursuit, armed with her sandal.

In the 1970s, Rialto used to invariably be full with hordes of people thronging the ticket window, and black marketing of tickets was quite common. 'But even during a full-house, friends were accommodated,' narrates a friend who recalls watching *Qurbani* (1980) perched precariously on a stool in the aisle.

Tom Alter saheb, who was fond of Rialto, wrote a romantic thriller *Rerun at Rialto* that was published in 2001. During a candid moment in 2013, he disclosed his plans to make a film based on his book. 'I want to make a film based on this story.

---

[294]*The Mussoorie Advertiser*, 9 June 1947, Vol 5, No. 8, Mussoorie: Mussoorie Art Press.

We will renovate Rialto for the film shoot,' he disclosed.

Rerun at Rialto was based on a love story that blossomed in the 1970s when a young girl falls in love with Chandu—a man who worked at the ticket window at Rialto. Cupid strikes, but the girl's family returns after their summer sojourn at Mussoorie. Decades later, the ageing lovers meet again at Rialto; meanwhile, there is a murder and Allan Kohli, a Mussoorie native but now a policeman, returns home after ages and is after the murderer.

'I want to cast Manoj Kumar and Sharmila Tagore in the lead roles. Both are wonderful artists and both have given their consent,' Tom saheb had told me.

'And what about me? Will you offer me a role,' I quipped.

'Don't worry, I will cast you too. You will be the English-speaking manager of Rialto,' he had replied with a twinkle in his eyes.

Tom saheb, maybe we will do a *Rerun at Rialto* in our next life!

Majestic Cinema

Majestic was the second cinema to come up in the town in 1921–1922. Located at the other end of the Mall, below Christ Church, Majestic was meant to cater to residents from the west-end of the town.

I remember it as the most ill-maintained cinema hall—torn seats, creaking fans, a hazy screen and seedy crowd. But perhaps things were much better in the 1940s and the cinema hall claimed to have the 'best sound and light in town.'[295]

In its heydays, Majestic also catered to Indian kings and princes. There was a 'royal box' located right next to the projector room, which was offered to royalty for private viewing. The royals were ushered into the 'box' through a separate entrance without having to pass through the 'crowd'.

Majestic, later named 'Vasu', continued to operate even after all other movie halls were shut down. After its closure, around

---

[295]Ibid.

Upcoming movies at Majestic cinema hall in August 1947. The 1935 classic Les Miserables is scheduled for screening on August 7. Incidentally, this was apparently the last film produced by Twentieth Century Pictures after which it merged with Fox Film Corporation to form 20th Century Fox. (Source: The Mussoorie Advertiser, 4 August 1947, Vol 5, No. 16, Mussoorie: Mussoorie Art Press)

2010, it was revived by three of my friends—Sandeep Sahni, Rajat Aggarwal and Rajat Kapur—a few years ago. Rechristened as The Ritz, the single hall has been converted with a multiplex with two smaller movie halls.

A projector from Majestic has been put up for public display on the Mall Road. This projector, with a label about the history of cinema in Mussoorie written by yours truly, remains our sole connection with the glorious days of cinema in Mussoorie.

Palladium Cinema Hall

Has anyone heard of a hotel with a full-sized cinema hall within its premises? That too in the early twentieth century! Ask any old timer of Mussoorie. 'Yes! Hakman's Hotel in Mussoorie had a cinema hall,' would be the immediate reaction.

Hakman's Hotel, the entertainment hub of the town until the 1970s, housed the Palladium movie hall since 1925. It is named after the famous 2,286-seater London Palladium (1910). Palladium changed to 'Capitol' after the ownership of Hakman's changed in 1946. Post-independence Capitol was well-known for screening English movies and there were three daily shows: 2.30 p.m., 6 p.m. and 9.30 p.m.

The movie hall was operated till the late 1970s, but once its projector and the sound system gave way, its doors were permanently shut.

Upcoming movies at Capitol cinema hall in August 1947. The name of this cinema hall had changed from Palladium to Capitol just a year ago in 1946. (Source: The Mussoorie Advertiser, 4 August 1947, Vol. 5, No. 16, Mussoorie: Mussoorie Art Press)

Roxy and Basant

Basant cinema (later *La Anjuman*) came up near The Rink, around the same time as Rialto. Roxy cinema hall was built opposite Basant cinema in 1943–1944. The name was, yet again, borrowed. This time, it was named after the colossus 6,000-seater Roxy Theatre of New York. The Brits surely lacked imagination; a movie hall in Calcutta had the same name as well.

Roxy was known for screening some of the best Hindi movies of that era. Old timers recall that *Nargis* (1946), starring superstars Nargis and Rehman, drew large crowds at the cinema.

Basant was also referred to as The Plaza in the 1940s. It was closed in the 1980s. The courtyard outside the building has become a convenient parking spot for local residents. A massive fire consumed Roxy in the 1960s, and later a hotel with the same name replaced the cinema.

The Rink

It seems that the owners of The Rink did not mind making some extra bucks. In the 1920s and 1930s, the skating rink was converted into a makeshift cinema. A temporary screen was put up at one end of the rink, while chairs were put up inside the skating rink. But as the number of cinema halls increased, this practice was discontinued. Boxing and wrestling tournaments were also organized frequently at The Rink.

As the audiences were drawn to the cinemas, several restaurants opened in the vicinity. There was Queens Restaurant and Milk Bar, located near Basant and Roxy, which served kebabs, korma, murgh musallam, cutlets and curries along with milk shakes. Grover's Corner House, opposite Picture Palace, was famous for 'Masala Dosha' and 'Baker's Bread', as well as 'Indian and English dishes'.[296]

---

[296]*The Mussoorie Advertiser*, 1 July 1946, Vol 4, No. 11, Mussoorie: Mussoorie Art Press.

But most famous was Kwality restaurant, just outside the entry to Rialto cinema. A Chinese chef, Mr Soon, was renowned for preparing authentic Chinese cuisine, while Kwality's special three-in-one ice cream always remained in huge demand.

Indian independence led to the exodus of the British and the merger of princely states, and that brought about a change in fortunes for the cinema halls in Mussoorie. Despite their skewed balance sheets, most cinemas managed to stay afloat till the 1980s, until the rising burden of entertainment tax and growth of the video industry finally brought the curtains down. All that remains today is crumbling buildings hiding rows of empty seats and memories of better times.

14

LAUTERBRUNNEN OF HIMALAYAS

'What are the places to visit in Mussoorie?' is the most obvious question posed by casual visitors. Local residents, particularly hoteliers and shopkeepers, vouch being subjected to this innocuous query innumerable times.

Kempty Falls is invariably the first recommendation. With over half a million visitors per year, Kempty Falls is the most visited tourist spot around Mussoorie, and rightly so. Barring the clutter of shops and occasional traffic congestion, it is undoubtedly the most splendid waterfall around Mussoorie.

But I have always insisted, and will continue to persist, that there are several other waterfalls in the town—maybe not as grand as the Kempty Falls—but quite picturesque nevertheless.

'Tourists only speak about Kempty Falls, and now Bhatta Falls is appearing on the tourism map. What about the others?' I quizzed my friend who was also a member of the Uttarakhand Tourism Board. 'We have so many waterfalls, at least six that I can count,' I added.

'It's about ease of access, I guess,' he replied sadly. 'Kempty already has a motorable road; one has also been developed at Bhatta Falls recently, but other waterfalls are too remote to suit the present breed of SUV-loving tourists,' he opined.

A bitter truth indeed. Present day tourists are in a hurry it seems—arriving on Fridays and departing on Sundays, without the time to explore new locations, or to hike to places not connected by motor roads. But visitors are not to be blamed entirely—our citizenry, our authorities and our local administration have also failed to promote other picturesque waterfalls in and around our town.

I believe Mussoorie is to the Himalayas what Lauterbrunnen[297] is to the Alps. Our town should also be known as the 'town of waterfalls'. Apart from Kempty, which is a cut above the rest, we have several other waterfalls, although smaller in size but less spoilt and definitely more tranquil than Kempty Falls.

Kempty

The saga started in the mid-1830s, when John Mackinnon, an educationist-turned-brewer, went out for a stroll or for a shikar (perhaps the latter) and encountered a magnificent waterfall barely a few miles from his house. The waterfall soon became a favourite haunt—not just for Mackinnon, but the entire citizenry.

A view of Kempty Falls in 1905. (Photographer: C. Nickels)

Ringal stream plunges down almost five-hundred feet to form this amazing waterfall—the largest around Mussoorie. A motor road bisects the waterfall; the portion above the road is more serene and calm, while the one just below the road sees the stream plunging down several hundred feet.

In 1902, the Britishers planned a hydro-power project here to generate electricity for Mussoorie, but the ruler of Tehri, under whose territory this fall was located, gave them the boot.

---

[297]Lauterbrunnen, a small municipality in Switzerland, is popularly known as the town of waterfalls. This narrow valley, nestled in the Alps, has at least seven major waterfalls that are tourist attractions.

Ultimately, the hydro-power project was shifted to Bhatta Falls, and our beloved Kempty lived to fight another day.

British trekking parties—venturing northwards towards Yamuna and beyond—frequently camped in the vicinity of the sparkling and gushing waterfall to add to the numerous 'tea' parties being organized by the residents.

Indian gentry having a picnic at a waterfall in the 1940s. It seems that this is the upper part of the Kempty Falls.

Did the tea-loving British originally name it 'camp tea' then? A rather contentious topic, especially with the senior historians of our town. This theory is often discounted on the grounds that there is a village nearby named Kempty (perhaps the fall was named after this village).

Many years ago, I got a call from a childhood friend. 'I have sent you something special by post,' he exclaimed. I eagerly awaited his letter, which arrived shortly. Inside was a hurriedly scribbled note, 'Did you like it?'

I was furious and immediately called him up. Hurling choicest abuses that we had honed in school, I hollered, 'Is this some joke? This is not even the month of April.

'You were a "tube light" then and it seems you are still the same. Look on top of the envelope,' my friend chuckled.

It was then that I was able to spot a ₹5 stamp of Kempty Falls affixed to the envelop. I was ecstatic—Kempty Falls had finally made it to the national stage. This stamp forms part of a series of four stamps on the 'waterfalls of India', the others being Athirappilly Falls (Kerala), Jog Falls (Karnataka) and Kakolat Falls (Jharkhand).

The stamp of Kempty Falls released in 2003.

Mossy Falls

Speaking about the waterfalls of the town, local residents do mention Mausi Falls near Barlowganj. Try asking them, 'Whose mausi[298] fell here?' and these local guides will scowl at you.

Actually, 'Mossy' did fall here. The story goes that Mr Moss (nicknamed Mossy), owner of Himalaya Bank, once happened to go on a picnic with the Hearsey family to these waterfalls. Poor 'Mossy' lost his footing at the waterfall and fell into the water, amidst roars of laughter by his companions. So the

A view downstream of Mossy Falls (circa 1949). (Picture courtesy: St. George's College, Mussoorie)

[298]'Mausi' is a Hindi word that means sister of one's mother.

name of Mr Moss was eternally etched in time as this waterfall came to be known as 'Mossy Falls'. But it is pronounced as 'Mausi Falls' nowadays—I'm sure Mr Moss squirms in his grave each time the name is mispronounced.

Part of the way to the falls is motorable; one needs to walk only about one kilometre to reach the waterfall. The falls emerge from a high precipice and presents a pretty picture, although the flow of water is a little relaxed as compared to other falls of Mussoorie. The surrounding trees form a sort of canopy, which looks exquisite, thereby contributing to the loneliness and the beauty of the falls. Venturing downstream, there's a small Shiva Temple and a Shivling, and a surge of water falls on top of the Shivling.

But be sure to pronounce the name correctly—or you might encounter an irate Mr Moss at the waterfalls.

Bhatta Falls

Undoubtedly another delightful waterfall is the Bhatta Falls, though not as grand as the Kempty, but more serene and secluded—although tourist footfall is on the rise. The fall derives its name from the nearby Bhatta village.

The Kyarkuli stream drops around 100 feet, forming this brilliant waterfall. The stairs alongside the fall can take one right up to the top from where one can capture some magnificent vistas. Below the waterfall, the fast-moving stream provides a wonderful opportunity to wade in the shallow water. India's second hydro-power plant is located at Galogi, a short distance downstream.

In the nineteenth century, this waterfall was a favourite amongst the 'boys' of the Masuri School who had also constructed a swimming pool here.[299]

---

[299]Hawthorne R., *The Beacon's Guide to Mussoorie* (Mussoorie: The Beacon Press, 1890), 10.

Connected by a motor road, and also recently by a ropeway, Bhatta Falls is worth a visit.

Jharipani Falls

This one is my personal favourite! Located on the outskirts of Mussoorie near Jharipani, the waterfall is about two kilometres from the main road, accessible halfway by vehicles, followed by a pleasant trek up to the waterfall. The cascading waterfall is the perfect place for nature lovers and hikers.

The falls are located in a remote area with towering mountains and a quaint jungle offering tourists a splendid view of nature. The falls emerge from overhead rocks, cascading down about 50 feet to form a shallow pool ideal for waddling.

The gushing sound of the waterfall, accompanied with the sweet melodious chirping of birds, the cool wind, the eccentric quietness of the place and the balmy sun overhead makes this waterfall an ideal spot for a day off. The surrounding forest stretches over miles, and sightings of junglefowls, bird and wildlife are quite common.

Hardy Falls

In the late 1860s, when students of Maddock's School[300] led by their popular principal Mr A.O. Hardy stumbled upon a waterfall below the south-western spur of Vincent Hill, they dutifully christened it Hardy Falls.

'And lest the world would not accept the students' christening, they labouriously carved the name in a rock by the fall, and time has not effaced it.'[301]

But had it not been so named by the boys, after my solitary

---

[300]Located at the site of present-day Savoy Hotel.

[301]The Rambler, *A Mussoorie Miscellany* (Mussoorie: Mafasilite Press, 1936), 95.

visit to the waterfall, I would myself have named it Hardy Falls—considering the hard time I had in reaching it. Hardy Falls is rarely visited owing to its difficult approach, but those accustomed to challenging hikes may enjoy an outing to the falls.

Murray Falls

Discovered by Dr Murray, a physician at the Landour Cantonment, the Murray Falls are also difficult to approach. Situated below Woodstock School, beyond Dhobi Ghat, the falls make a pretty picture as a stream drops nearly 150 feet over a precipice. While a fine sight during the rains, the fall is reduced to a mere trickle during the dry summers.[302]

Approachable only by a long trek, these falls are rarely visited.

The stream on which these falls are located meanders down the valley to reach Sahasradhara near Dehradun—where a sulphur spring is located. Dr Murray had discovered the sulphur spring and 'sent a number of ailing soldiers from the Landour Depot to benefit by what he considered healing powers of these waters.'[303]

---

[302]Northam J., *Guide to Masuri, Landaur, Dehradun and The Hills North of Dehra* (Calcutta: Thacker, Spink and Co., 1884), 47.

[303]Bodycot F., *Guide to Mussoorie* (Mussoorie: Mafasilite Printing Works, 1907), 63.

15

YOU'VE GOT MAIL

Mobiles, e-mails and WhatsApp have almost driven away the postman from our doorsteps. Armed with the power of technology and instant communication, we refer to the post as 'snail-mail'. As I try to remember, it seems like eternity has passed since I last mailed (not e-mailed) a letter, or purchased a stamp, or simply entered a post office.

Modern technology is making post offices redundant. But technology cannot snatch away the fond memories of eagerly waiting for the postman to deliver a letter from a loved one or bring a money order, an admission letter from a college or even a job appointment letter. It can also not erase the history of post offices indelibly etched in the sands of time.

The history of post offices in Mussoorie is as old as the town itself. Bits and pieces such as a postmaster who was the father of the most famous hunter-conservationist of the world, hosting the only post office in the country still housed inside a hotel's premises with a seal still bearing the name of the hotel and the anecdote about a former prime minister who sent letters to his daughter during his prolonged stay in Mussoorie further romanticize their glorious history.

First Post Office

A post office at Landour, established as early as 1827, gave Mussoorie its first address. Captain Young, the founding father, is believed to have used his influence to get the post office set up to 'serve' the British soldiers recuperating at the convalescent depot in Landour.

We often talk about last-mile connectivity, but the challenge for the postal department was connectivity over the last 'seven miles' between Rajpur to Mussoorie.

It was the 'dak runners' or 'harkaras' who made the postal movement possible. These lowly paid Indian workers—armed with a long stick and carrying post on their back—trudged barefoot up and down the steep slopes. It took between two to three hours for these fast-walking foot messengers to carry the post from Mussoorie through Landour–Barlowganj–Jharipani to Rajpur, where 'dak ghari' or horse drawn carriages picked up the post.

'Since posts were carried on foot there must have been delays in delivery,' I conjectured during a conversation with my friend and noted philatelist Mr Abhai Mishra.

'Not at all. Perhaps the system back then was much faster,' he countered.

'I am sure that's not true.'

'Yes, it is,' Mr Mishra said, showing me an old envelope.

A letter sent to Reverend Morrison at Dehradun from Mussoorie on 30 September 1891. The postmarks on front and back cover indicate that letter was redirected to Himachal and then again to Dehradun and was delivered on 3 October. (Images courtesy: Collection of Mr Abhai Mishra)

The envelope dated back to 1891. The postmark showed that on 30 September 1891, a letter was sent to a Reverend Morrison in Dehradun from Woodstock School, Mussoorie. The delivery of the letter was attempted on 1 October but it was found that the Reverend had moved to Subathu near Solan in Himachal Pradesh. Instead of returning the letter to Woodstock, it was redirected to Solan, where it reached the very next day. Delivery was attempted on the same day (i.e. 2 October 1891). By that time, the Reverend had decided to return to Dehradun and so the letter was sent back to Dehradun and was successfully delivered to the Reverend on 3 October.

'Can you get such efficiency nowadays?' my friend questioned.

And all this for just a half anna[304] (a little over 3 paisa) postage! For those who think that this was just a one-off example, let me share another one, again from Mussoorie.

It so happened that on 28 July 1902, an invitation was sent by a certain 'The Happy Valley Christian Endeavour Society' to a resident, Miss Sharpley. It was an invite to attend the weekly club meeting at 5 p.m. the same day. The postcard regarding the invite was posted at 1.45 p.m. on 28 July and was delivered at 4.30 p.m. in the evening. Given the half an hour's notice, I am sure Miss Sharpley would have been able to reach the meeting. Thanks to the prompt service by our postal department.

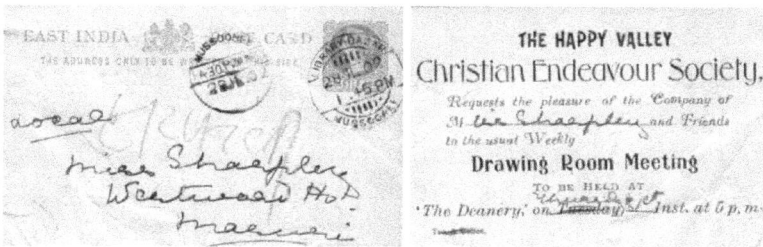

Front and back cover of the invitation sent by Christian Endeavour Society to Miss Shapley. Notice the stamps on the front cover–letter posted at 1.45 p.m. and delivered at 4.30 p.m. (Images courtesy: Collection of Mr Abhai Mishra)

---

[304]An 'anna' was a unit of currency used in India during the British colonial era. An anna was equivalent to 1/16 of a rupee, making it equivalent to 6.25 paise. The anna was discontinued as a currency unit in 1957.

During the years 1858–1862, Christopher William Corbett was the postmaster at Landour Post Office. Does the surname 'Corbett' ring a bell? Let me elaborate, Christopher was the father of legendary hunter-turned-conservationist Jim Corbett. He married his lady love Mary Jane Doyle at Mussoorie and, in 1862, the couple migrated to Nainital.

Landour Post Office remained the head post office of Mussoorie during the nineteenth century until it was shifted to Rorleston House on the Mall in Kulri in 1909, while the one at Landour was made a sub-post office.

Sub-post Offices

The Post Office Act (1837) gave the British the exclusive right to send letters in the territories controlled by the East India Company, resulting in a surge in the number of post offices. In 1871, a sub-post office was opened at Charleville Hotel to cater to the needs of guests, followed by another one at Barlowganj in 1893 (for St. George's College), at Jharipani in 1901 (for Oak Grove School), while in 1902, another sub-post office came up in the Savoy Hotel premises at Library market.

Ask any old student of St. George's or Oak Grove about the importance that the post offices at Barlowganj or Jharipani had for them. 'After arriving at school, we could not meet our parents for months; phones and emails were non-existent, so letters were the only medium of communication. I used to drop at least one letter every week to my parents, and each time I passed through Barlowganj, I would drop into the post office to check if I received a reply,' recalls Prashant Anand, an alumnus of St. George's College.

The Charleville and Savoy sub-post offices were perhaps the only post offices in the country to be set inside hotel premises— ostensibly since the who's who of society stayed in these hotels. Rudyard Kipling, Pearl S. Buck, His Holiness the Dalai Lama were amongst those who used the services of these post offices.

Pt. Jawahar Lal Nehru wrote a number of letters[305] to his ten-year-old daughter Indira[306] in 1928. At that time, Ms Indira was spending her summers in Mussoorie,[307] and Mr Bhardwaj tells me that she was staying at the home of her aunt Mrs Vanchu—the house was located just below Savoy Hotel. Meanwhile, Pt. Nehru was at Allahabad. This exchange of thirty-one letters was facilitated through the Savoy Post Office, which faithfully served the Nehru-Gandhi family since 1914, when Pt. Jawahar Lal Nehru wrote a letter to his mother Swaroop Rani while staying at a cottage called Craig Top at Mussoorie.

Charleville Post Office bore the seal 'Charleville', but after the property was acquired by the government to establish a training academy for civil servants in 1959, the seal was changed to 'NAA'.[308] In 2009, to commemorate fifty years of the academy, a commemorative postage stamp was also issued.

A stamp of LBSNAA released in 2009.

---

[305]Nehru J., *Being a Brief Account of the Early Days of the World, Written for Children* (later published as Letters from a Father to His Daughter) (Allahabad: Allahabad Law Journal Press, 1929).

[306]Former Prime Minister of India, the late Indira Gandhi.

[307]'These letters were written to my daughter Indira in the summer of 1928 when she was in the Himalayas at Mussoorie and I was in the plains below.' Excerpt from the foreword written by Pt. Nehru for his book. Nehru J., *Being a Brief Account of the Early Days of the World, Written for Children* (later published as Letters from a Father to His Daughter) (Allahabad: Allahabad Law Journal Press, 1929), ix.

[308]National Academy of Administration, which is now known as Lal Bahadur Shastri National Academy of Administration.

Meanwhile, the Savoy Post Office continues to be housed in a building owned by the Savoy Hotel, the monthly rental for which is a paltry ₹99—rent being fixed prior to Independence and not enhanced since. Apart from its picturesque location and century-old legacy, this post office has a unique seal.

The picturesque sub-post office within the premises of Hotel Savoy.

Postmaster Gaurav Joshi enlightened me that usually a seal at a post office bears the name of the place and the name of the head post office—by this logic, the seal at Savoy should have been 'Library, Mussoorie'—but the century old seal here has a print that reads: 'Savoy Hotel'.

The sub-post office at Jharipani, located just outside the gate of Oak Grove, continues to battle on, but sadly, the one at Barlowganj was shut down several years ago to be replaced by a hotel. Lack of 'economic viability' also sounded the death knell for Landour and Savoy sub-post offices in 2020 when authorities decided to close down these historic institutions. However, after much persuasion by yours truly and a few like-minded residents, the decision to shut down these post offices was junked. These historic landmarks got a lease of life for now.

The century old seal of the sub-post office that reads 'Savoy Hotel'.

The Simpleton and the Post Box

The shiny red post boxes installed on the roadside remained a source of intrigue for the simple village folks who frequented Mussoorie. Such a tale was once recounted by a friend of my grandfather's many years ago when I was a teenager.

Mr R[309] was a dear friend of my grandfather's, and both buddies used to while away their afternoons playing rummy and sipping tea. A jolly and chirpy person by nature, Mr R was famous for playing innocent pranks whenever any opportunity arose.

One afternoon, my grandfather handed me a letter to post as Mr R, holding cards in his hands, gazed at me and smiled.

His smile sent alarm bells ringing. 'Is anything wrong, Dadaji?' I asked cautiously.

He shook his head. 'Nothing wrong, just wondering whether

---

[309]It is my practice to mention the names of people only after their due permission. Since Mr R passed away several decades ago, I am refraining from disclosing his name.

you know where to post this letter,' he remarked.

'Of course. The post box is just down the street,' I replied proudly. 'Why do you ask?'

Apparently satisfied with my reply, he looked at his cards and blurted, 'Run along boy; once you return, I will tell you a very interesting story.'

The story that he narrated subsequently went like this:

Around the 1920s, a simpleton from a rural background arrived in Mussoorie and found employment at a fruit shop in Landour. The shop was adjoining the Landour Post Office.

Whenever he got time, he used to sit outside the shop, gazing at his surroundings in awe, observing the mannerisms of townsfolk, particularly of Englishmen and English women. He was quite intrigued by the gleaming red box outside the post office. Often, he would see British ladies and gentlemen approach this box and drop something inside through the small gap at the top of the box.

This piqued his curiosity. '*What is this box meant for? What do these gora saheb and memsaheb drop into the red box?* he often wondered.

Then one day, a mischief-monger explained to him that it was a British custom not to litter on the streets and that they dropped waste into this box.

While working at the fruit shop, our simpleton was able to lay his hands on a few apples and bananas each day. He decided that whatever fruits he ate, he would deposit the leftovers in the red box.

And from the next day onwards, when the postman came to collect the mail, he would find banana peels and apple cores inside the post box.

After this happened for several days, the infuriated postman complained to the postmaster. A police complaint was made and a constable was asked to keep watch and apprehend the offender.

Noticing frequent visits to the postbox by the village emigrant made the constable suspicious, and our simpleton was arrested and taken to the police station. After a tight slap from the constable, the fruit shop worker tearfully revealed that he was just doing his 'duty' of disposing garbage properly.

The simpleton was let off with a stern warning. However, this incident gained wide publicity.

'I was a young boy of your age when my father told me about this incident,' Mr R said as he summed up the story and picked up his cards to resume his game of rummy.

16

DIGGING FOR GOLD AT THE OLYMPICS

I once happened to bruise my knee badly after falling on the abrasive bajri (gravel) filled ground at St. George's College. 'What nonsense! Can't we have proper grounds in our school rather than these bajri bowls?' I cursed.

I pleasantly came to know several years later that these 'bajri bowls' in St. Georges' College and also in nearby Oak Grove School had been the breeding ground of hockey champions— players of the highest calibre who had won several Olympic golds.

During the era when the Indian hockey team was dominating the world stage, winning successive Olympics under the leadership of 'the wizard' Major Dhyan Chand (1928–1936), several players from Mussoorie were ably assisting the legend in his quest to amass gold for the country.

As many as ten players from the schools of this hill town had made it to the Olympics—and not just made it, they went all the way to win gold! The 1928 Indian Olympic team had six players, the 1932 team had five players and the 1936 team had four players who had studied in Mussoorie.

'Did these rough and uneven surfaces help our hockey champions in gaining better ball control?' I sometimes question.

Amsterdam Olympics–1928

- George Marthins, St. George's College
- M.A. Gateley, St. George's College
- W.J. Goodsir-Cullen, St. George's College
- R.J. Allen, Oak Grove

- B.E. Pinniger, Oak Grove
- L.C. Hammond, Oak Grove

Los Angeles Olympics-1932

- C.C. Tapsell, St. George's College
- R.J. Allen, Oak Grove
- B.E. Pinniger, Oak Grove
- L.C. Hammond, Oak Grove
- R.J. Carr, Oak Grove

Berlin Olympics-1936

- C.C. Tapsell, St. George's College
- E.J. Goodsir-Cullen, St. George's College
- Lionel C.R. Emmett, St. George's College
- R.J. Allen, Oak Grove

The first team fielded by India (a British colony then) in the Olympics was in 1928. Jaipal Singh led the team that included the great Dhyan Chand. Nearly half the team comprised former students of Mussoorie schools: Broome Eric Pinniger (vice-captain), George Marthins, Maurice A. Gateley, William J. Goodsir-Cullen, Richard J. Allen and Leslie C. Hammond.

In the run-up to the tournament, the Indian team thrashed the English team 4-0, after which the scared Brits promptly withdrew their team from the Olympics. Perhaps wanting to avoid the humiliation of losing to their 'colony'.

The Patrician Brothers-run St. George's College (estd. 1853), among the oldest schools of Mussoorie, nurtured seven champions, six of whom represented India and one represented England. From St. George's College, Mussoorie, George Marthins (1928), Maurice Anthony Gateley (1928), William James Goodsir-Cullen (1928), Carlyle Carrol Tapsell (1932 and 1936), Ernest

John Goodsir-Cullen (1936) and Lionel Charles Renwick Emmett (1936) were part of the gold-medal-winning Indian hockey teams.

Marthins (1905–1989), who played as a left or right winger, formed a formidable combination with Dhyan Chand during the Amsterdam Olympics in 1928. The duo scored 19 goals out of a total of 29 goals scored by the Indian team. Marthins found the net five times.

In a crucial match against Belgium, India was in a spot of bother, as Belgium deployed almost half their team to mark Dhyan Chand. Dhyan Chand broke the marking through short passes to Marthins or Feroze Khan, who were able to score easily. India won that match 9-0: Khan 5, Marthins and Dhyan Chand 1 each.

Maurice Gateley, who played as a left or right winger, etched his name in history when he scored the first Olympic goal for India on 17 March 1928.

The Goodsir-Cullens were amazingly-talented siblings who played in the midfield. William Goodsir-Cullen (1907–1994) played in the defence as well as in the midfield; it is believed that due to his 'rock-solid' defence, our team did not concede a goal during the Amsterdam Olympics. His younger brother, Ernest Goodsir-Cullen (1912–1993) was an outstanding half back who played for the country in the Berlin Olympics. Post-independence, Ernest settled in Ireland in 1952—a forty-five-year-old Ernest received frantic requests to play for the Irish team in the 1952 Olympics. He was a qualified doctor but had to re-qualify for the medicals in Ireland and could not play in the 1952 Olympics due to his final examinations.

Lionel Emmett—a schoolmate of Ernest's—was also part of the hockey team in 1936. Emmett played as a forward.

Tapsell (1909–1975) played in the defence during the 1932 and 1936 Olympics. While Dhyan Chand, Ali Dara and Roop Singh were tormenting the opposition, it was Tapsell who thwarted opposition counter-attacks. He also scored a goal during the tense final at Berlin against the Germans.

N. Nugent was another St. George's alumnus who studied here prior to Independence and later became part of the bronze-medal-winning team of Great Britain at the 1952 Helsinki Olympics.

The alumnus of Oak Grove School included Richard James Allen (1928–1936), Eric Pinniger (1928 and 1932), Leslie Charles Hammond (1928 and 1932) and Richard John Carr (1932).

Eric Pinniger (1902–1996), perhaps the most talented of the Mussoorie lot, was regarded among the world's best centre half's. He was also the vice-captain of the 1928 team and went on to lead the team in the Olympic finals.

'I heard that Eric Pinniger, who was still the best centre half in the hockey world, and who captained India towards the end of the 1928 Olympics, expected to be chosen as captain. It was reported in the press that Eric had declined to make the trip when he was not made the captain. Later I learnt that Charles Newham, one of the founding officials of the Punjab Hockey Association, and then on, the staff of the Lucknow-based newspaper *Pioneer*, successfully persuaded Eric to revise his decision,' Major Dhyan Chand writes in his autobiography.[310]

Pinniger became the vice-captain in the 1932 Olympics as well, but opted out of 1936 due to some feud with the management. He was urgently recalled after India suffered a humiliating defeat in a pre-Olympic match but he never rejoined. Pinniger was an excellent marksman too—but missed competing in Antwerp Olympics (1919) as India failed to send a team.

Richard Allen (1902–1969) has the unique distinction of being a triple gold medallist in Indian hockey. He was a terrific goalkeeper who conceded only three goals in the three Olympics that he played.

After the 1936 Olympic finals, there was a report in *The Hindu* describing the brilliance of Tapsell in the defence and Allen at the goal post: 'The vigorous German attacks were brilliantly saved

---

[310]Chand D., *GOAL* (Chennai Sport & Pastime, 1952), 4.

by Allen and Tapsell. The goal scored by Weiss [of Germany] was the only goal scored against the Indians throughout the tournament. The whole Indian team put up a splendid display. Dhyan Chand and Dara impressed by their combination, Tapsell by [his] reliability and Jaffar by his tremendous bursts of speed.'[311]

Richard Carr was part of the 1932 Olympic team; he played in the forward position and scored a goal in the lone match he played at the Olympics. Carr also represented India in men's 4×100 metres relay in the same Olympics.

Leslie Hammond figured in two Olympic games as a defender. He played three matches in 1928 and one in 1932.

The names of these champions still resound on the playgrounds of St. George's College, where the four houses in the school are named after these illustrious pupils and great stalwarts: Marthins, Cullen, Gateley and Tapsell. The railways-managed Oak Grove School has also named a field after Eric Pinniger.

With football mania catching the fancy of students, hockey is now rarely played on those fields in St. George's and Oak Grove where our champions had learnt to pick up the hockey stick.

---

[311]'Dhyan Chand shines in Berlin as India bags third straight Olympic hockey gold', *The Hindu*, 16 August 1936, https://sportstar.thehindu.com/hockey/india-wins-third-successive-hockey-gold-medal-1936-berlin-olympics-dhyan-chand-independence-day/article32359207.ece

ACKNOWLEDGEMENTS

This book is an outcome of the support extended by innumerable people over several years that it took me to write this book.

First and foremost, I would like to seek the blessings of my late grandfather and father, who had inculcated in me an interest in the history of Mussoorie by sharing interesting facts and information. They also left behind several old documents, guidebooks and photographs that helped me in writing this book.

I would like to thank my wife, Neha, who has been a pillar of strength during the course of writing this book. She read early drafts, provided honest feedback and was a constant source of motivation. My nephew Vinayak, an excellent writer himself, was my sounding board. He would read the book cover to cover, suggest changes modestly and, at times, even edit the text and share it with me for my comments. Not to forget my son Anant, who it seems is a budding historian himself. He browsed through many old journals, helped me generate QR codes that are included in this book and also helped in scanning and editing the photographs.

Next, I would like to thank the master himself, Ruskin Bond, for his guidance and for sharing several interesting anecdotes, as well as noted authors Bill Aitken and Stephen Alter.

I must thank the eminent travel writer duo Hugh and Colleen Gantzer for valuable insights about the town and historian Gopal Bhardwaj for sharing the most important bits of the town's history.

A special word of thanks is reserved for Sunil Arora of the famous Cambridge Book Depot, who was a constant source of encouragement and guidance.

I am indebted to Vineet Aggarwal, CEO of Hotel Savoy, for

sharing photographs of Mussoorie from their archives for use in this book and Richard and Jennie Swetenham of the Swetenham family, whose ancestors owned the Cloud's End Estate, for sharing old family photographs.

I also thank Pramode Sawhney, owner of Mussoorie Art Press, for kindly sharing copies of old editions of *The Mussoorie Advertiser*—clippings of which have been used in this book.

I am also grateful to Atul Sethi, an author himself and Uttarakhand Bureau Chief of *The Times of India*, who provided valuable guidance regarding book publication and Megha Adhikari, also of *The Times of India*, for editing some chapters of the book.

I am much obliged to distinguished philatelist Abhai Mishra for sharing pictures of old letters that are used in this book, and to Deepak Rawat for helping me with the photographs.

And lastly, I would thank the entire team at Rupa Publications, especially Dibakar Ghosh.

QR CODES

The coordinates of some of the places discussed in this book are provided to the readers in the form of QR codes. These codes can be scanned using Android or iOS devices in order to get the locations on Google Maps.

Scanning QR Codes on Android devices

- Open Google Lens or any other external QR Scanner app
- Scan the QR code
- On scanning the QR, a link will pop up
- Click the link, which will then take you to the Google Maps location of the QR you scanned

Scanning QR Codes on iOS devices

- Open the Camera app
- Scan the QR code
- On scanning the QR, a link will pop up
- Click the link, which will then take you to the Google Maps location of the QR you scanned

LANDOUR CANTONMENT

Char Dukan

Mullingar

Pari Tibba

Sisters Bazaar

CLOUD'S END AND NEARBY LOCATIONS

Cloud's End

Bhadraj Temple

George Everest House

Surveyor's Stone

Wishing Well

CAMEL'S BACK ROAD

Camel Rock View Point

Ropeway to Gun Hill

Scandal Point

The Rink

CHURCHES

Christ Church

Kellogg's Memorial
Church

Methodist Church

St Paul's Church

St Peter's Church

Union Church

CEMETERIES

Camel's Back Road
Cemetery

Landour Cemetery

Roman Catholic
Cemetery

SCHOOLS

CJM Hampton Court

CJM Waverley

Oak Grove School

St George's College

Woodstock School

Wynberg Allen School

HOTELS

Charleville Hotel (now LBSNAA)

Hakman's Grand Hotel

Hotel Himalaya

Savoy Hotel

BANKS

Alliance Bank of Shimla

Himalaya Bank and
Imperial Bank

CINEMA HALLS

Picture Palace

Vasu Cinema

WATERFALLS

Bhatta Falls

Jharipani Falls

Kempty Falls

Mossy Falls

POST OFFICE

Head Post Office Mussoorie

OTHER LOCATIONS

Dhanolti

Galogi Power House

Galogi Ropeway

Ice Well

Municipal/Company Garden

Mussoorie Library

www.ingramcontent.com/pod-product-compliance
Lightning Source LLC
Chambersburg PA
CBHW020441100426
42812CB00036B/3407/J